OPENING THE TOOLBOX

Unlocking Curriculum's Potential

John Maempa
with Sandy Friesen

Gospel Publishing House
Springfield, Missouri
02-0531

ISBN #0-88243-833-6

Contents

Preface

There are many elements that go into a successful classroom experience, but three stand out in my mind. There must be an effective teacher, a receptive student, and a subject matter to be taught. The material in this training book focuses on the last of these elements.

Teachers throughout the years have tried a variety of ways to collect subject matter to present in the classroom. Some teachers try to create a new and fresh lesson on their own from the pages of the Bible each week. These individuals often tire of this approach or find themselves fixed on a particular topic for months on end. Other teachers select various books, articles, and videos and attempt to be creative as they present material from the minds and hearts of popular writers. This approach has mixed results, but often there is little forethought about biblical balance and direction. The majority of Sunday School teachers use curriculum that they purchase from their fellowship or from a local bookstore. Many teachers express frustrations concerning their curriculum and some even feel overwhelmed by its content.

Opening the Toolbox: Unlocking Curriculum's Potential is written with the teacher who uses curriculum but feels a little frustrated with it in mind. The goal of the authors of this book was to anticipate the key questions teachers ask about curriculum and to provide practical answers that will make the curriculum more useful to them and assist them in becoming more successful in the classroom. Some of the questions addressed in this book include: "Curriculum: Why Do I Need It?" "How Is It All Put Together?" "What Are All the Parts For?" "How Can I Make It Fit?" "How Can I Make It Work?" and "Why Is a Pentecostal Curriculum Important?" In addition, Maempa uses the last chapter of this book to answer various "frequently asked questions" that don't warrant an entire chapter. The result is the fine book that you now hold in your hands.

John Maempa brings a wealth of experience to his role as editor-in-chief of Radiant Life Resources. He spent many years in curriculum development before moving on to become the managing editor of his fellowship's premiere weekly magazine. From there he accepted the position of editor of his fellowship's missions magazine before returning to Radiant Life Resources to give general oversight to curriculum production. In addition to Maempa's professional qualifications to write this book, he has served for many years as a Sunday School teacher in a local church which uses the curriculum his department produces each week. He knows firsthand the challenges of adapting curriculum for the local church setting as well as the benefits of a systematic and well-planned presentation of the gospel which curriculum can provide.

Maempa enlisted the assistance of the Radiant Life curriculum staff specialist, Sandy Friesen, to write the important chapter on learning styles. Friesen has taught extensively in this area and provides a very practical chapter that will have many applications in your classroom.

This project could not have come to completion without the able assistance and coordination given to it by Gospel Publishing House's Book Editing staff and Product Development team.

It is our hope that *Opening the Toolbox: Unlocking Curriculum's Potential* will provide you with the kinds of answers you need to maximize the investment your church has made in curriculum and in you.

Clancy Hayes
Training Coordinator
Sunday School Department

Curriculum:
Why Do I Need It Anyway?

It's the Sunday before you begin a new quarter and your Sunday School superintendent has just handed you the usual stack of materials—a teacher guide, several student books, a resource packet, and a handful of take-home story papers. You're grateful for the resources because they help you know what to teach and how to teach week after week; but now that you've been teaching for several years you're asking yourself, *Is all this material really necessary?* In fact, you've seen the same basic themes cycle around at least two times since you started teaching. Maybe you could save the church money by drawing on your experience and creating your own materials, or maybe you want to try other curricula. Or you may feel that it is unnecessary to use a printed curriculum; all you need is the Bible.

On the other hand, you may be brand-new at teaching Sunday School and have no idea whether these materials really are what you want or need. *Are there other options I should explore?* you wonder. If you have been struggling with these issues or you simply want to know more about the value of

Sunday School curriculum to your teaching this chapter and the ones that follow will help you.

Staying on Course

Picture a runner crouched low to the ground, feet placed squarely against the starting blocks, eyes gazing intently ahead. His muscles are tense in anticipation of the race. Only one thing is on his mind—breaking the tape at the finish line. At the sound of the starting pistol, the runner springs into action, pouring every ounce of energy into the contest. Running along the prescribed track, the athlete strides toward the goal.

So what does that scene have to do with curriculum?

The illustration actually provides the backdrop from which the word curriculum is derived. *Curriculum* is rooted in the Latin word *currere*, which, when translated, means "to run." The image portrayed is a racecourse or a prescribed path for running a race. Implied is the fact that reaching the goal requires following a set course until the finish line is reached. Obviously, to win the race, you have to stay on course.

Curriculum, whether used in public education or in Christian education, is designed to help learners reach specific learning and developmental goals. Information organized and presented in a way that fits the characteristics of the students helps them run along the course until they have successfully reached the goal.

In Christian education a spiritual dynamic is absolutely vital to success. Not only does learning take place in a course of study, but lives are changed as believers develop in accord with the principles of God's Word.

Perpetuating Truth

But is it really necessary to have all those teacher guides, student books, and other resources to help children, youth, and adults reach the goal?

From the time humans first began to codify truths, principles, and ideas in written form, instructional materials have been in use. Whether on papyrus scrolls or rice paper, teachings have been passed along for generations. Even from ancient times, before much of Scripture was available in handwritten form, leaders of Israel's families were reminded of the need to convey truth to succeeding generations. "These commandments that I give you today are to be upon your hearts," Moses declared. "Impress them on your children. Talk about them when you sit at home and when you walk along the road, when you lie down and when you get up. Tie them as symbols on your hands and bind them on your foreheads. Write them on the doorframes of your houses and on your gates" (Deuteronomy 6:6–9).

The psalmist Asaph also focused on the importance of perpetuating essential truths. "We will not hide them from their children," he wrote; "we will tell the next generation the praiseworthy deeds of the LORD, his power, and the wonders he has done . . . so the next generation would know them, even the children yet to be born, and they in turn would tell their children" (Psalm 78:4,6).

Perpetuating truths, ideas, and principles is the fundamental purpose of any instructional system, whether by word of mouth from one generation to the next or through the use of prepared resources. Without a carefully planned, systematic strategy for teaching, it is difficult, if not impossible, for the Church, individually and corporately, to stay on course. Resources—instructional tools—that closely adhere to God's Word and provide meaningful application to life, help guard against the distortion of truth and departure from the faith. They keep us from running out of bounds and getting lost somewhere in the periphery.

The purpose of this book is to open the toolbox of Radiant Life resources that are available to teachers involved with Early

Childhood through Adult classes. As you work through this study, you will better understand how these tools can help your students victoriously reach the finish line.

A Historical Perspective

On the heels of the great Pentecostal outpouring at the turn of the twentieth century, thousands of new Spirit-filled believers felt compelled to take the gospel to the ends of the earth. Others were zealous to plant churches stateside and share what they had experienced in the great outpouring—true indicators of the Holy Spirit's presence and power. However, no training systems were in place, nor was there much in the way of published material that could help guide the fledgling group of Pentecostals.

As the new Pentecostal movement began to spread and increase in fervor, early leaders quickly realized the need to provide both organization and instruction. Each was viewed as essential to conserving the harvest and to proclaiming and preserving sound biblical teaching and Pentecostal distinctives. Without careful instruction and leadership, the possibility for error in biblical interpretation was great.

E. N. Bell, a pastor in Malvern, Arkansas, was already printing a monthly periodical called *Word and Witness*. In Plainfield, Indiana, J. Roswell Flower was distributing the first Pentecostal weekly called *The Christian Evangel*. Eventually the two publications merged and became *Today's Pentecostal Evangel*. Though no formal organization was yet in place for the Pentecostal believers, these early leaders recognized the importance of providing instruction and guidance to any who would read and heed.

Prior to the formation of the General Council of the Assemblies of God in April 1914, in Hot Springs, Arkansas, a special call for a general conference was issued through the *Word and Witness*. Among five purposes listed for the gathering, the delegates would be asked to consider that "[since] the Gospel should be taught, preached and published in all the world before His return, we should consider the Ministerial, School and Publishing interests, to the glory of God."[1] During that formative meeting, both E. N. Bell, who was elected general chairman of the council, and secretary-elect J. Roswell Flower, agreed to turn their publications over to the newly formed Fellowship. By the time the second General Council was called in November of that same year, *Word and Witness* and the *Christian Evangel* were already circulating a combined total of 25,000 issues. Both helped to bring a sense of cohesiveness and direction to the infant Fellowship, demonstrating the power of print communication. The careful teaching conveyed in those early publications helped the fledgling Fellowship stay on course.

During the November council, a landmark decision was made to set aside five thousand dollars "for publishing equipment to be owned and controlled entirely by the General Council and to be used for the glory of God."[2] Though the equipment was primitive by today's standards, efforts were soon under way to provide additional training materials beyond the periodicals already being printed.

By 1919 the newly formed Gospel Publishing House was printing simple lesson leaflets and quarterlies for primary, junior, intermediate, and adult students. Eventually, story papers were produced that would further help Pentecostal believers, young and old, understand the gospel and the importance of Spirit-filled living.

Ad copy appearing in the April 7, 1928, *Pentecostal Evangel* reads as follows:

"Our Pentecostal Little Folks"
A four-page paper for Beginners. Contains the Sunday
School lesson and helpful stories for little folks. Well illustrated. Just the thing to introduce little minds to the reality
of the gospel and the things of the kingdom of heaven.

"Our Pentecostal Boys and Girls"
A four-page weekly paper prepared for the purpose of
bringing the full gospel to our boys and girls. Each
number is well illustrated. Biographies of noted
Christians, missionary letters, the Sunday School lesson,
testimonies of healing, and helpful stories by Pentecostal
writers are special features of this paper.

"Gospel Gleaners"
Our new adult Sunday School paper is very attractive. Full
of helpful and interesting things prepared for the young
people's and adult classes, it supplies a long-felt need.

Though basic in their appearance, these early publications helped form solid biblical and doctrinal foundations for a new generation of Pentecostal believers.

Today's curricular materials are processed through sophisticated electronic editing and imaging equipment and a state-of-the-art press, but the mandate remains unchanged—to provide biblically sound teaching materials that guide both teachers and students in a thorough, Spirit-empowered, life-changing understanding of God's Word.

Mandate for Sound Teaching

As the athlete runs the race, success depends not only on speed, but also on careful pacing and staying within the closely defined boundaries of the racecourse. To try to cover ground too quickly would result in loss of energy. To ignore the boundaries would mean veering completely off course. In both letters to his young protégé in ministry, Paul urged Timothy to be wary of false teachers, to avoid getting caught up in meaningless debates and endless arguments. He warned that "in later times some will abandon the faith and follow deceiving spirits and things taught by demons. Such teachings will come through hypocritical liars, whose consciences have been seared as with a hot iron" (1 Timothy 4:1,2). Does that remind you of things we're facing today?

Paul urged Timothy to focus on the essentials, to "command and teach" the principles of salvation (see vv. 9–11) and to "devote [himself] to the public reading of Scripture, to preaching and to teaching" (v. 13). Paul further admonished Timothy, "Watch your life and doctrine closely. Persevere in them, because if you do, you will save both yourself and your hearers" (v. 16). In short, Paul encouraged Timothy to stay the course and not allow other influences to distract him from going for the goal.

Paul knew that Timothy was convinced of the truth because he had heard it taught from infancy from those whom he knew and trusted (see 2 Timothy 3:14,15). He reminded Timothy that Scripture is "God-breathed and is useful for teaching, rebuking, correcting and training in righteousness" (v. 16). Today the same process takes place in Sunday School classrooms as teachers demonstrate God's love and convey the principles and truths of His Word to children, youth, and adults. In the context of the Sunday School classroom, students are able to become engaged in the learning process through hearing, seeing, and doing. The ultimate goal is that they, like Timothy, will become convinced of the truth, internalizing it for themselves.

A Christian Worldview

Teaching, applying, and modeling eternal truth are vital to helping students of all ages grasp, internalize, and live the Christian life. In his book *How Now Shall We Live?* Charles Colson writes, "Our choices are shaped by what we believe is real and true, right and wrong, good and beautiful. Our choices are shaped by our worldview. . . . The basis for the Christian worldview, of course, is God's revelation in Scripture."[3] Yet Colson stresses further that it is not enough to know what Scripture teaches and to go through the motions of Christian living. Instead, all believers must understand that Christianity is ultimate reality, that our relationship with Christ must affect all we think, say, and do.

While important matters of Christian living are conveyed from the pulpit, much of the line upon line, precept upon precept is laid within the context of the Christian education program of the local church. There truth, theology, doctrine, and their application to life are measured out to students in accord with their stages of development and levels of understanding. In an environment conducive to inquiry and reflection, students are helped to understand that God's revelation touches all areas of life, that they are responsible for more than knowing and feeling, that they must act on what they know and feel.

Of utmost concern is helping students be able to state what they believe and why they believe it in intelligent and compelling ways. Society's postmodern mind-set is not satisfied with platitudes and pat answers. Many people are desperately hungry for truth but do not accept the Bible as the authoritative rule of faith and conduct. Postmoderns generally don't see the Bible as authoritative. Many reject that Jesus is the Son of God. Nor do they even believe God created the heavens and the earth. Without careful teaching, Christian children, youth, and adults are ill equipped to address these challenges.

Life-Related Learning

In the latter part of the eighteenth century, Sunday School teachers focused primarily on conveying Bible knowledge and leading students to Christ. Both are very important, but little emphasis was given to applying Bible teaching to real life. Today, relating Bible content, evangelizing, and applying the Word to life are all important elements in the Christian education process. In the early childhood through early elementary years, major emphasis is given to learning content. Children learn the basic stories of the Bible and begin to practice, in a child's level of understanding, the life principles of those stories for today. As the students move into the preteen years

16

and above, stronger emphasis is placed on relating the Bible to life and translating what is taught into action.

Instructional Approaches

But to help transmit truth to life, biblically sound, compelling presentations are needed to engage students in the teaching-learning-applying process. How this is accomplished depends on the instructional approach used. Obviously, choosing the right approach to teaching is vital to helping those in life's race stay on course and finish the race successfully.

Three basic approaches can be found to teaching and to choosing instructional materials: (1) teaching directly from the Bible text using no other resources, (2) teaching from self-prepared curriculum, and (3) teaching from a printed curriculum. Is there a best approach? Let's look at the choices.

1. *Teaching from the Bible text.* Without question, some gifted teachers can teach directly from an open Bible. Their years of study and experience have resulted in a thorough knowledge of Bible content. They have gathered compelling illustrations and anecdotes along with other resources that help make the passages come alive. This approach is most common in young adult and older adult classes, although it can be used at any age level.

While any approach to Christian education must first and foremost be Bible-centered, some shortfalls are inherent with teaching from the biblical text alone. Among them is the tendency to stay with the favorite and the familiar. Certain books and passages of the Bible are easier than others to teach and apply to daily living. Difficult texts may be overlooked even though they contain important truths and principles. Exposure to a broad range of Scripture is important to building a firm foundation of biblical understanding.

Teaching directly from the Bible also lends itself primarily to a lecture or auditory approach to instruction, with little or no interaction from the students. Unless the students privately engage in in-depth study of the passages before class, there is little frame of reference for questions and discussion. Additionally, though many expository teachers are well versed in the content of the passages presented, some have little experience with developing meaningful methods for student interaction or are uncomfortable with that approach to teaching. Without interaction, students can shift into neutral mentally and simply accept what they hear without giving serious consideration to the impact the Scripture passage has or should have on their lives. Student engagement in the learning process is important at all age levels.

Closely related shortfalls are the matters of correct Bible interpretation and the integrity of doctrinal or theological concepts presented. Again, unless the students study beforehand or have some kind of printed resource to which they can refer, they are at the mercy of the teacher's grasp of the passages being discussed. While most teachers will have done their homework in these areas, others may be inclined to pass along private interpretations of Scripture that may or may not be credible. In his second letter to Timothy, Paul urged his young friend to be one who "correctly handles the word of truth." He warned Timothy to "avoid godless chatter, because those who indulge in it will become more and more ungodly. Their teaching will spread like gangrene" (2 Timothy 2:15–17). They are the ones who have wandered away from the truth.

2. *Developing one's own curriculum.* Second, some Christian educators choose to prepare their own curriculum. Without question, some teachers are able to expend a great deal of creative energy to provide lessons, life applications, and even supplementary resources that engage students in the learning process. While motivation may be to save cost or to tailor instructional materials more closely to the local situation, some shortfalls are inherent with this approach as well. Chief among them is the sheer amount

18

of work that preparing a meaningful, well-balanced, age-level-appropriate curriculum requires.

During his college years, a teacher of middle school boys became disconcerted with the printed curriculum and decided to present some topics "of interest" to his boys for a change of pace. Considering himself an innovative teacher and knowledgeable in a number of areas, he thought this would be a creative approach. Presenting two or three possible topics, he invited the students to choose one, which they did. The next day, standing amid the stacks of books in the college library, the teacher realized the ominous task he had just given himself. Already pressed by his busy college schedule, he would now have to spend hours researching and developing from scratch a series of lessons week after week. What had seemed like a great idea quickly dissolved into a grand impossibility.

As with teaching directly from Scripture, writing one's own curriculum can lead to the tendency to stay with the favorite and familiar. In some cases curriculum developed by church staff or volunteers is limited to a certain set of lessons that are repeated over and over, with little attention given to providing a balance of themes and broad Bible coverage. Additionally, privately developed resources, though possibly strong in content, are often lacking in compelling and creative supplementary materials.

3. *Teaching from a printed curriculum.* A third option is to use a prepared curriculum such as Radiant Life. While a printed curriculum should never be viewed as a crutch to make teaching "easy," well-written teacher guides, student books, and supplemental resources greatly enhance both preparation and presentation. A carefully planned scope and sequence provides a balance of Bible narratives, doctrinal themes, and contemporary issues presented in age-level-appropriate ways.

Of course, any printed curriculum needs to be adapted to the local situation. There are no one-size-fits-all curricula on the market. Classroom size, number of students, age-level groupings, budget allowances, and level of teacher experience among other factors will determine what resources will work best and how they will be used in the classroom. No curriculum publisher should expect slavish adherence to every part of the material. In every teaching situation there must be room for the teacher's creativity as well as for the spontaneous intervention of the Holy Spirit who sometimes directs in ways that differ from the teacher's plans. At times, special "teachable moments" arise that are unique to a particular class or individual student. While those cannot be planned in a printed curriculum, the materials provide a framework of study and application that may give rise to those teachable moments.

Overall, a well-planned printed curriculum that upholds the biblical and doctrinal distinctives of the Church will serve well. Using such materials will ensure as much as possible the communication of essential truths to students of all ages. While there are numerous choices in curriculum that can be considered, great care must be taken to protect against influences that prevent students from receiving a well-rounded overview of all Scripture—the "whole counsel of God."

The Curriculum Quest

Of the many curricula on the market, some are published by denominations and others are prepared by independent publishing enterprises. Not all are created equal. This is evident not only in the level of creativity and innovation the curricula reveal; more important, it is evident in the arena of the Pentecostal distinctives. Foremost among those is the issue of Spirit-filled living, including, but not limited to, the doctrine of speaking in tongues as the initial physical evidence of the baptism in the Holy Spirit. Non-Pentecostal curricula do not present the gifts of the Spirit as relevant for our day. If referenced at all, the doctrine of divine healing and other evidences of the miraculous are handled from a purely historic "it happened back then" perspective. The faith of our children, youth, and adults must be stirred to believe for the miraculous today. They must be encouraged toward a Pentecostal experience in order to have power to witness and serve. It is vital that students receive a broad exposure to all of God's Word and the doctrines that form the foundation of our faith.

One pastor relates the following experience in a church that had been using a variety of curricula in its Sunday School program:

> As I reviewed applications for church membership, I was happy to see that a number of our young people wanted to join the church. But I became concerned as I noticed each had responded "no" to the question, "Have you been baptized in the Holy Spirit?" Their explanations were also identical; they didn't understand what it was about.
>
> Nearly all of them had been raised in the church and had attended Sunday School for the last ten years. *So why don't they understand one of our major doctrines?* I wondered.
>
> Then I remembered. Ten years before, some teachers in our younger classes wanted to switch to a different curriculum. Their reasons seemed justified. The other materials were well written and had many good qualities. So we switched to Brand X. I assumed the teachers would work in our doctrines at appropriate times.
>
> Ten years later, the bottom line told the sad story—it didn't work. Brand X failed us not because of what it said, but because of what it didn't say. And we reaped the results.
>
> Some materials on the market offer terrific features, but remember, the terrific can never replace the important.

Someone has said that two factors influence the rise or fall of a denomination or fellowship—its colleges and its Sunday School curriculum. Unfortunately, by the time a student is in college, it is often too late to correct misconceptions if doctrinal distinctives have not been carefully communicated throughout his or her formative years in Sunday School. Departure from those distinctives can be avoided by using a curriculum that clearly articulates the fundamentals of the faith from early childhood through adulthood. The demise of Pentecost is only one generation away. Failure to convey the essentials of the faith particularly to children and youth is guaranteed to result in deviation from the foundational truths of the Church.

The challenge for every publisher, including Gospel Publishing House, is to provide materials that are not only biblically and doctrinally sound and offer a balance of themes and issues. The materials must also be compelling, appealing, and cutting-edge in their appearance and instructional design. Combining the "essential" with the "terrific" is the goal.

Evaluating Curriculum

Here are some important questions to ask when looking at any curriculum package:

- *Is it Bible-centered?* As indicated earlier, that is a foremost consideration. Even when dealing with contemporary issues and themes, curriculum must be centered on God's Word.
- *Is it accurate?* Is the Word "correctly handled" (see 2 Timothy 2:15)? Accuracy of interpretation and application are essential to helping our students stay on course. Accuracy is also important when dealing with facts about history, geography, science, and so on. Teachers must be able to rely on the integrity of the materials they are using.
- *Is it user-friendly?* Does it lend itself to the teaching style of today's busy but dedicated teachers through easy-to-locate information, clearly outlined directions, and simple, enjoyable activities?
- *Is it relevant?* Does the curriculum deal with issues that students are facing in our world today? Though written thousands of years ago, God's Word speaks clearly and

authoritatively to contemporary issues.

- *Is it age-level appropriate?* A well-designed curriculum package is developed according to the mental, physical, emotional, social, and spiritual characteristics of each age level. The complexity of lesson presentations and the suggested activities are adjusted in accord with those characteristics.
- *Is it doctrinally sound?* Do the resources carefully present the doctrines of the Church? The importance of this cannot be overstated. Doctrinal teachings form a foundation of faith that will give students a firm footing in a postmodern culture that continually challenges the Christian life and experience. Balance in handling the doctrines also is important.
- *Is it visually appealing?* Do the student materials, visuals, take-home papers, and other resources provide compelling graphics and illustrations that capture attention? Do the design and format help convey the content of the lessons?
- *Is it cost-effective?* This is a vital concern, especially in churches with limited budgets. Is the cost of the material equivalent to its value in the teaching/learning process?
- *Does it work?* Does it offer a variety of methods that can be used to reach the variety of learning styles of students so they can retain the information and apply the concepts to their lives?

Each of these questions is kept in focus in the development of Radiant Life resources produced by Gospel Publishing House. Biblical and doctrinal integrity, age-level appropriateness, relevance, instructional design, and other issues are intentionally addressed quarter by quarter. Colorful student books, visuals, posters, and other resources dynamically engage the students in the teaching/learning process. Compact discs enhance lesson presentations through music, skits, and various resources that can be downloaded on computers. All materials are developed with age-level characteristics and learning styles in mind. God's

Word and its application are measured out in accordance with the students' ability to comprehend.

Facing the Challenge

While creative and innovative resources are important to the Christian education process, the ultimate concern is to stay the course regarding biblical and moral absolutes and doctrinal distinctives. The erosion of absolutes and challenges to faith in Jesus Christ will become exponentially greater as we move further along the Great Commission time line. "For the time will come when men will not put up with sound doctrine," Paul warned his young associate Timothy. "Instead, to suit their own desires, they will gather around them a great number of teachers to say what their itching ears want to hear. They will turn their ears away from the truth and turn aside to myths" (2 Timothy 4:3,4). Never before has there been a more crucial time for believers who are "prepared to give an answer to everyone who asks [them] to give the reason for the hope that [they] have . . . with gentleness and respect" (1 Peter 3:15).

Yet even with careful teaching, we can become sidetracked in our run for the goal. In his letter to the Galatian believers, Paul scolded the church for getting caught up in arguments about the Law's requirements that no longer applied. "You were running a good race," Paul wrote. "Who cut in on you and kept you from obeying the truth?" (Galatians 5:7). A correct understanding and interpretation of God's Word are important to staying on course.

Children, youth, and adults must be taught precisely what God's Word teaches. All who have opportunity to teach and disciple must continue to clearly mark the path of biblical understanding and truth. That is the only thing that will keep those we instruct from being sidetracked by the spiritual, moral, and ethical challenges of our day.

24

Also using the analogy of a race, the writer to the Hebrews urges us to "throw off everything that hinders and the sin that so easily entangles, and let us run with perseverance the race marked out for us" (Hebrews 12:1). The path is clearly lined for those who are taught the principles of God's Word and pay close attention to them. Sin so easily entangles, but as students are engaged in an intentional, systematic study of Scripture and determine to heed its teaching, they will finish the race. They too will be able to say with Paul as he neared the end of his race, "I have fought the good fight, I have finished the race, I have kept the faith. Now there is in store for me the crown of righteousness, which the Lord, the righteous Judge, will award me on that day—and not only to me, but also to all who have longed for his appearing" (2 Timothy 4:7,8).

Curriculum resources alone will not bring about spiritual growth and formation in students' lives. Even though carefully developed by Spirit-filled writers and editors, their use will not automatically bring about life transformation and help students face the challenges of living in a postmodern world. Yet these resources can be vital tools to use in the process of helping learners come to a full understanding of God's Word and His will and purpose for their lives. That's why you need them.

The ultimate goal of Christian education is to help develop Christlikeness in the lives of students, not only to teach, but to disciple them as well. When this is done, students in our Sunday School classes will be able to "run in such a way as to get the prize" (1 Corinthians 9:24).

As you continue your study, make your own commitment to faithfully convey the Word of God to the students under your charge. Pray that the Holy Spirit will not only guide you into all truth, but also that in turn you will be able to guide those you teach in the way that leads to life everlasting.

Endnotes

[1]*Word and Witness*, February 1914.

[2]*General Council of the Assemblies of God Minutes,* November 1914.

[3]Charles Colson and Nancy Pearcey, *How Now Shall We Live?* (Wheaton, Ill.: Tyndale Publishers, Inc.), 1999, pages 13,14.

How Is It All Put Together?
Understanding the Curriculum Development Process

Have you ever stood at the base of a towering skyscraper and marveled at its beauty, size, and architecture? Peering upward, scanning the glass panes and the outer skeleton of concrete and steel, you wondered how such a massive structure was built. What you saw, of course, was the finished project. Hidden from view were thousands upon thousands of details needed to complete the building. Long before the building was erected, all those elements were drafted in a master plan, or blueprint, that showed exactly where every room, window, door, staircase, and light switch should be, along with myriad other details. Constructing the building properly required following the blueprint in detail.

Spiritual formation also requires following a plan—God's plan. While the students in your classroom already have been formed physically, they are in a continual process of spiritual and moral development. How effectively that development takes place depends a great deal on how well they understand and apply God's Word to their lives. Helping that developmental process take place is the central purpose of curriculum development.

The Master Blueprint

As a Christian educator, you are very familiar with the Master Blueprint for life—the Bible. The inspired Word of God is the revelation of God to humans and our authoritative rule of faith and conduct. Its instructions must be followed carefully to ensure proper spiritual formation. To fully understand the Master Blueprint, however, it is helpful to break it down into a series of other blueprints that will help children, youth, and adults effectively learn its facts, truths, and principles and how to apply them to life. In a sense, book studies, topical themes, and contemporary issues arranged into quarterly and unit themes are like blueprints that help convey the Bible's content in ways that will help build lives spiritually. Understanding the truths and principles of God's Word is vital to spiritual formation and growth. Therefore, it is important that curriculum resources provide a systematic, intentional progression of topics and themes that help students of all ages grow in their understanding of the Master Blueprint and follow God's plan for their lives.

Scope and Sequence

Radiant Life curriculum development is guided by a "scope and sequence" chart that lists quarterly and unit topics and themes covering a broad scope of studies. The themes and topics are "spiraled" in a carefully designed age-level sequence. Study content moves from very basic information and concepts to more advanced ones as students progress through various stages of mental and spiritual development. This does not mean, however, that major concepts and truths are presented only at one point in the progression and not at other points. Rather, spiraling allows various concepts and truths to be revisited at various stages in the progression so that students can enter the teaching-learning process at any time in their lives and receive instruction on many basic, fundamental truths that are important to their spiritual development. Not only are the concepts and truths repeated as they spiral, but also the approach to those studies advances from basic knowledge of key facts to application and analysis.

For example, consider a lesson on Noah. Here are possible emphases from early childhood through adulthood:

Early Childhood	Early Elementary	Upper Elementary	Youth & Adult
• There was a man named Noah	• Noah loved God	• God found Noah faithful	• Noah was faithful and righteous
• Noah loved God	• Noah was obedient	• Noah cared about other people	• Noah obeyed God regardless of what others thought
• Noah built a boat	• Noah followed God's plan	• Noah's obedience pleased God	
• Noah obeyed God	• Obedience pleases God	• God is merciful	• God is a merciful God
		• God cares for those who obey Him	• God cannot tolerate sin
		• God punishes evil	• Opportunity for salvation can be lost
			• We must tell others about Christ before it is too late

Each instance illustrates that objectives are spiraled as the age level progresses to address more complex issues and applications.

Curriculum Goals

The blueprints are age-level appropriate, presenting basic details in the early childhood and early elementary years. These become more complex as the students advance to higher levels. Facts, principles, and truths are measured out to students from infancy through adulthood. The scope and sequence are developed with specific age-level learning and developmental goals in mind.

Early Childhood

Curriculum designed for children 0–12 months provides topics and themes that initiate spiritual formation during the early months of physical, mental, emotional, and social development. The curriculum is designed to introduce foundational biblical truths to babies from birth until the time they begin walking. Loving relationships, enjoyable hands-on activities, conversations, and songs help form the roots of love, trust, and obedience—three important foundations of Christian faith. Topics and themes presented help little ones begin to understand the concepts of God's love and care, family relationships, the created world around them, and the marvel of their own bodies as God's creations.

For toddlers and 2-year-olds (12 months–2 years), careful effort is made to nurture positive attitudes about the Bible, Jesus, friends, the Church, and the importance of family. Children also are exposed to key Bible characters, such as Joseph and Zacchaeus. Teaching methods reinforce the development of love, trust, and obedience introduced in Radiant Baby curriculum. Loving relationships and intentional repetition of guided play activities, teacher-guided talks, and simple songs introduce children to foundational Bible truths. And age-appropriate questions are designed to teach the students strategies for Bible-based problem solving.

Preschool materials for children ages 3–4 years provide active learning through hands-on activities. Children are introduced to many familiar Bible stories from both the Old and New Testaments. Topics include stories about Moses, Elijah, Paul, Bible heroes, and others. Children practice biblical principles as they interact with one another to act out the Bible stories, to make crafts and snacks, to help take care of their part of the church, etc. An emphasis on Pentecost is initiated at this level when children learn how God helped Peter preach on the Day of Pentecost. Again, intentional questions lead the students into applicational thinking.

Specific Early Childhood learning goals include the following:

- to prepare each child for the experience of new birth in Jesus
- to help each child know that the Bible is a special book from God that tells about God and Jesus
- to foster in each child a tender spirit and a sensitive attitude toward God
- to help each child become aware that God made and loves him or her
- to help the child feel secure in the knowledge that he or she is important to God
- to help each child feel that he or she is part of the church
- to help each child develop foundational concepts, habits of living, and patterns of conduct that will help him or her apply Christian principles to every relationship of life

Early Elementary

As children move from preschool years into the school-age years, the building blocks of learning include more of the Bible narratives along with some topical themes. In Kindergarten curriculum (ages 5–6) and Primary materials (ages 7–8, grades 1–2), children are given an understanding of basic Bible stories and Bible truths. The Early Elementary curriculum is designed for life change as the children apply the Bible to their lives. The curriculum provides teaching ideas geared to the spiritual, physical, mental, social, and emotional development of children ages 5–8. These enable teachers not only to convey important facts and principles from God's Word, but also to evangelize and disciple the children.

Unit themes in the Kindergarten curriculum include stories about Joseph and Joshua, Bible heroes, the first church, and Jesus as Savior and Healer. In the Primary materials, unit themes include Abraham and his family; the Church, worship, and service; Israel's wilderness wandering; and Paul's missionary journeys.

Overall goals for Early Elementary curriculum include the following:

- to teach one age-level Bible story each Sunday
- to help each child learn a lesson-related Bible verse each Sunday
- to help children learn how to apply each Bible lesson to their lives
- to provide teachers with practical, usable, hands-on lessons
- to encourage teachers to lead children to Christ
- to encourage children to live for Christ

Upper Elementary

As children progress through their elementary years, more emphasis is placed on topics and themes that help children understand how to apply their Christian experience to life. In Middler curriculum (ages 9–10, grades 3–4), students are exposed to unit themes dealing with attitudes, witnessing, and spiritual growth. At the same time they are learning more about Jesus, God, and the person and work of the Holy Spirit. More emphasis is being placed on the reality of Pentecost, and children are encouraged to seek the baptism in the Holy Spirit. The upper elementary years are prime years for this experience. Receiving the Holy Spirit's empowerment will give them the ability to stand for Christ and be a witness in the more turbulent teen years that are not far away.

Preteen curriculum (ages 11–12, grades 5–6) continues applicational and doctrinal emphases with themes on right choices, personal will, the work of the Holy Spirit, the baptism in the Holy Spirit, and spiritual gifts. Other themes focus on major components of Bible content, such as the books of the Law, history, poetry, the Gospels, and so on. Careful effort is made to help students not only build their foundational understanding about the Bible, but to put Bible knowledge into practice through a personal relationship with Jesus Christ. They are encouraged to demonstrate that relationship through Christian living, witnessing, Bible study, prayer, and church involvement.

Overall goals for Upper Elementary curriculum include the following:

- to lead students to accept Christ as Savior
- to teach Bible principles for daily living
- to provide appropriate doctrinal emphases
- to guide life application of Bible lessons through questions, role-play, open-ended stories, activities, and puzzles
- to present God's Word in ways that are visually appealing and appropriate for the abilities of the age level
- to enhance memorization of God's Word through games and other interesting activities
- to encourage daily Bible study and prayer
- to challenge students to lead a Spirit-filled life

Youth

Youth curriculum is designed to build on the foundation established through earlier years in Sunday School. Basic doctrine and familiar Bible stories are reviewed in new and innovative ways so students will not feel they have heard it all before, yet newcomers will be able to grasp basic spiritual concepts. Teens will discover how the Bible relates to contemporary life and will learn how to apply biblical principles to daily issues they face.

Through Young Teen (ages 13–15, grades 7–9) and High School resources (ages 16–18, grades 10–12), teens study topics such as spiritual warfare, feelings, emotions, sexuality, faith and works, tough questions, attitudes and responsibility, and cultural confrontation. Issues of personal revival, worship, and praise also are vital components in the youth scope and sequence. Both Old and New Testament book surveys and doctrinal studies are woven throughout.

Overall goals for Youth curriculum include the following:

- to lead students to accept Christ as Savior
- to teach and encourage students to understand the doctrines of the Bible
- to challenge students to seek and receive the baptism in the Holy Spirit and to explore the gifts and fruit of the Spirit
- to help teens learn to apply biblical principles to contemporary issues
- to teach familiar Bible stories in new ways to expose teens to a deeper and broader selection of biblical teachings
- to encourage personal and daily Bible study and prayer
- to help teens develop a biblical faith and encourage them to share their faith with others
- to present God's truths as exciting and relevant for today
- to disciple teens to lives of holiness and commitment to God
- to communicate God's changeless truths in contemporary words, styles, and designs so God's Word will not be perceived as something just for older people or little kids
- to challenge teens to practice biblical stewardship and effective Christian service

Young Adult

As construction workers complete the foundation, superstructure, wiring, and plumbing in a new building, many more hours are spent with the finishing touches. Building the door and window frames, installing the wallboard, tile, stair railings, carpeting, curtains, light fixtures, and much more must be done before the structure is complete. In a sense, the foundation and superstructure in Christian education are raised through the childhood and teen years. Finer detail regarding the infrastructure is addressed as students reach young adulthood and older adulthood.

Of course, as with many analogies, this one is limited. While a building is raised and the finishing touches completed, the process of building lives spiritually is never done. Throughout the teen years and adulthood, along with the finish carpentry and embellishments, there must be the shoring of foundations and maintaining and renovating the superstructure.

Curriculum for young adults examines the issues of our times and finds scriptural answers that can be applied to the lives of young adults, primarily in the college and early career stages of life. The emphasis of the curriculum falls on a translation of doctrine into contemporary, everyday application. Evangelism among family, friends, and coworkers is regularly promoted. Young adults are challenged to a pursuit of Christian growth. Teaching methodologies rely on group interaction, provocative questioning, and a personalized approach to biblical themes and narratives.

Young Adult curriculum can be used in a traditional classroom lecture style; however, it is also developed to follow the interactive adult Bible fellowship model. This approach allows for fellowship and guided group discussion. Emphasis is placed on the teacher or leader as a facilitator rather than lecturer. Some themes dealt with in the Young Adult resources include studies on the history of the Pentecostal movement, the Christian and sex, marriage commitments, crucial issues in the church, effective Bible study, and personal relationships. Studies are developed on a five-year cycle.

Overall goals for the Young Adult curriculum are as follows:
- to translate doctrine into contemporary thought and include supplemental material from current Christian magazines
- to provide biblical answers for the issues of our day and encourage consistent Christian living
- to encourage students to be baptized in the Holy Spirit and challenge them to lead a Spirit-filled life
- to point students toward Christian maturity through

personal prayer, worship, Bible study, self-discipline, and fellowship with other believers
- to motivate young adults to share the gospel as forcefully as they share their other views on life
- to present all of life as God's gift and the energy of youth as a resource to be tapped for ministry
- to teach that the Bible is the foundational guidebook for life and to encourage faithful Scripture study
- to encourage teachers to present the plan of salvation frequently

Adult

Adult curriculum emphasizes systematic Bible study to find scriptural answers that can be applied to adults in all stages of life. Gospel Publishing House curriculum is based on a seven-year cycle that includes studies from Genesis to Revelation. Quarterly and unit themes are developed through the cooperative efforts of the Pentecostal/Charismatic Curriculum Commission, which includes the Assemblies of God, Church of God (Cleveland, Tennessee), International Pentecostal Holiness Church, Pentecostal Church of God, and the Pentecostal Church of God of Prophecy. Although the cycle is repeated every seven years, different aspects of the Bible text are dealt with in each cycle. Evangelism among family, friends, and coworkers is regularly promoted. Adults also are challenged to continually pursue Christian growth and ministry. Teaching methodologies rely on group interaction, provocative questioning, and a personalized approach to biblical themes and narratives.

Overall goals for the Adult curriculum include the following:
- to translate doctrine into application for daily living in the various stages of adulthood and encourage consistent Christian living
- to point students toward Christian maturity through personal prayer, worship, Bible study, self-discipline, and

fellowship with other believers

- to encourage students to be baptized in the Holy Spirit and challenge them to lead a Spirit-filled life
- to motivate adults to share the gospel as forcefully as they share other views on life
- to present every stage of life as God's gift and all of life's experiences and possessions as resources for ministry
- to teach that the Bible is the foundational guidebook for life and encourage faithful study of the Scriptures
- to encourage teachers to present the plan of salvation frequently

Curriculum Cycles

A scope and sequence also indicates the yearly cycles for the various quarterly themes and age levels. For example, curriculum for infants is on a one-year cycle, for toddlers and two-year-olds it is on a two-year cycle, and for preschool it is on a three-year cycle, and so on. This essentially means that the quarterly themes presented are repeated again after one year, two years, or three years, depending on the cycle arrangement.

Does this mean everything is reprinted exactly as before? No. Each time a new cycle begins, the previous cycle's studies are reevaluated, revised, and updated. Responses from the field are given careful consideration, and in some cases various lessons are rewritten or restructured to update illustrations, learning reinforcement activities, or life applications. Visual aids, posters, work sheets, and other items in the resource packets are evaluated for maximum effectiveness. Continual updating and revising are the central advantages of a dated versus undated curriculum. With the latter, no changes or adaptations are made from one cycle to another.

Some teachers resist the concept of recycling curriculum, wanting completely new and different materials each time a cycle repeats. It is important to remember that, while the material is repetitious to some extent for the teacher, the students move on. After being exposed to the material in a given cycle, they proceed to the next level. Similarly, in secular education, children and youth are taught various subjects that will help them master more advanced concepts and information in succeeding grade levels. Each level of curriculum is carefully planned to provide a balanced treatment of topics and themes that will help students both better understand God's Word and grow spiritually.

Measuring Progress

In addition to formulating the broad scope and sequence for all levels of curriculum material, specific knowledge, response, and skill goals are outlined for each age-level period. Obviously, some goals are more easily measured than others. Some cannot be measured. However, as students progress from one level to another, there should be discernible benchmarks that show an increased understanding of biblical facts and truths and evidence of a real-life internalization and application of spiritual concepts.

So, what should children know by the time they have completed the various phases of their Sunday School experience? Some of the parameters listed reflect feelings, impressions, and cognitive understanding, while others pertain to issues of effective spiritual growth and maturity.

National guidelines have been established that indicate what children, youth, and adults should know about God, Jesus, the Holy Spirit, God's Word, sin, salvation, divine healing, the baptism in the Holy Spirit, the Second Coming, and a host of other biblical, doctrinal, and theological themes and concepts. These provide vital guidance to the curriculum development process.

For example, during the early childhood years, children from infancy through age 2 should be able to sense and understand the following.

Baby (0–12 months)
- sense that God is someone who loves them
- develop an appreciation of their bodies
- feel love and care
- begin to appreciate the wonder of God's creation
- begin to realize the importance of family

Toddlers and Twos (12 months–2 years)
- sense that God's house is a good place to be
- develop an appreciation for the family of God
- learn basic Bible stories about God, Jesus, Elijah, Peter, and Zacchaeus
- express appreciation for who they are, their families, and God's care for them
- gain a greater appreciation for the world God created

By the time children have completed their upper elementary years, they should have a well-established foundation of biblical knowledge, should have responded to what they know, and should have developed skills that will help them in the Christian walk and service. The chart which follows highlights this in relation to seven important areas of spiritual formation.

Strand	*Response and Application*
Personal Commitment • Salvation • Christian growth • Christian living	• Repent of sin • Accept Jesus as Savior • Have devotions • Pray • Attend church • Monitor attitude • Memorize and internalize valuable Scriptures or passages (Romans 3:23, 5:10, 6:23, etc.) • Learn to seek help from the Bible • Make decisions that please God • Apply Christian principles in every situation • Develop an attitude of worship and praise

Strand	Response and Application
Bible Knowledge	• Believe the Bible
• Inspiration	• Read the Bible
• Bible information	• Look to the Bible for answers
• Theology	• Study about the Bible
Δ Water baptism	• Be baptized in water
Δ Communion	• Take Communion, understanding its importance
• History	• Research the history of the Bible
• Writers	• Recognize the role each writer of the Bible played
• Key passages	
Δ Ten Commandments	• Give reasons for believing the Bible
Δ Lord's Prayer	• Know the books of the Bible in order
Δ Parables	• Locate passages and verses
Δ Parallel of the Gospels	• Use Bible helps effectively (concordances, dictionaries, atlases, maps, etc.)
	• State the doctrines of the Bible
	• Explain a passage in light of context
Christian Service	• Recognize the responsibility of the Great Commission
• Ministry	
• Missions	• See every situation as a ministry opportunity
• Careers	• View the world as a mission field
• Social gospel	• Examine ways you can reach out to others
	• Learn about various aspects of ministry
	• Learn about the world and effective ways to reach it
	• Look for ways to use your career as an outreach
	• Volunteer your time, money, prayers, etc.
	• Feed the hungry
	• Clothe the poor
	• Care for the sick

Strand	Response and Application
The Miraculous • Pentecost • The Holy Spirit Δ Fruit Δ Gifts Δ Work of • Miracles • Healings • Interventions • End times • Angels/demons	• Seek to receive the baptism in the Holy Spirit • Allow the Holy Spirit to work in your life to help you • Obey God • Develop the fruit of the Spirit • Expect miracles • Acknowledge that God has a plan • Acknowledge that Jesus will come again • Recognize that angels and demons are a part of the spiritual warfare that Christians face • Speak in tongues as the Spirit gives you utterance • Pray for the sick • Pray for miracles • Learn what it feels like to have the Holy Spirit leading you • Study end times • Recognize the signs of the times • Discern spirits as the Holy Spirit empowers
Life of Christ • Prophecies about Him • His childhood • His adulthood • His ministry • His teachings • His sacrifice • His family and friends • His culture • His miracles	• Accept Jesus as the Messiah • Recognize that God had/has a plan • Accept the complexity and the simplicity of what Jesus did for each of us • Study all aspects of Jesus' life • Think before you act and decide what Jesus would do in this situation • Study Jesus' culture • Learn about His miracles • Examine the parables of Jesus • Tell His story to others

Strand	Response and Application
Biblical Examples • Spiritual role models • The good and the bad • Longitudinal character studies (David as a child, teen, man, parent, leader, etc.) • Women	• Study the people of the Bible • Learn about what makes a good role model versus a bad role model • Examine cultural roles of people of the Bible • Tell about the life stories of a number of biblical characters • Apply what you learn from those characters to your life
About God • His character • His deity • God as Creator • God as Savior • God as Provider • God as Sovereign	• Study the names of God • Study the characteristics of God • Study the work of God in the people of the Bible • Examine God's sovereignty • Explore different ways God intervened • Examine God through the Old and New Testaments • Allow God to transform your life • Examine God the Father's role within the Trinity

Similar goals have been established for other levels of curriculum.

Measuring life change is more challenging than measuring learning goals. Often life change is not evident until years later. However, Radiant Life curriculum's emphasis on life application that encourages students to put into practice what they are learning can make evaluating life change easier. Lesson plans include reviewing what happened during the week prior and inviting students to share something they did to apply the previous week's study. Be sure to take time for your students to share what they have done. If that is done regularly, they will begin to sense the importance of actively applying the biblical concepts and truths they are learning.

42

Outlining and Writing

Once the scope and sequence and age-level philosophies and goals are in place, the curriculum development process then calls for preparing weekly lesson outlines and unit themes. In some cases an entire quarter (usually thirteen weeks) is devoted to a single theme; however, most quarters across the age-level spectrum are divided into two to four units. This provides variety in thematic development and broadens the spectrum of subject areas that can be covered in a given age level.

Study outlines feature the topic (title), objective, life application emphasis, key verse (or memory verses), and the various points for lesson content development. These provide guidance for writers of the curriculum. In most cases writers are assigned a unit of three to six studies to prepare. This usually involves preparing the teacher guide, student quarterly, and resource packet items.

When the studies have been written, they are submitted to a team of editors who read through all the materials, making sure the content corresponds with the outlines and other instructions given to the writers. In addition to streamlining or tightening copy and checking it for biblical and doctrinal accuracy, editors focus on how all components in the curriculum package correlate. Careful attention is given to discussion questions, activities, audio-visual helps, and student resources to be sure they are as effective as possible in the lesson presentation.

Providing the blueprints to help with the spiritual formation of children, youth, and adults is a complex task; yet the greatest test of their worth is in their effective presentation in the class-room and their application to real life. A blueprint has little value if left on a sheet of paper. However, when the instructions are conveyed and followed, something beautiful and functional is formed. So it is in the process of spiritual growth and development. As students of all ages receive instruction based on the

Master Blueprint and apply it to their lives, they will become mature followers of Christ and habitations of the Holy Spirit's presence and power, built on a firm foundation of faith.

Printed curriculum serves not only as a series of blueprints that reveal the building stages given in the Master Blueprint, but also provides specialized tools for you to use to help build lives spiritually. Each resource is carefully designed to fit the learning needs of the age level for which it is intended. Spiritual formation is aided as you handle the tools effectively. As you continue in this course, determine to use the tools you have been given to help your students grow spiritually.

What Are All the Parts For?
Understanding Curriculum's Essential Elements

Shopping for a sewing machine after using her old one for nearly twenty years, Sarah was amazed at the complexity of the new models. When she had purchased her old one, a buttonhole feature and zigzag stitches were pretty sophisticated applications. Now, as she looked over the selection, she found machines that looked like they belonged in Mission Control. Some had computer screens and more buttons and dials than she had ever seen. Not only could these high-tech marvels sew buttonholes and make zigzag stitches, they could be programmed to embroider intricate patterns at the touch of a button, and much more.

Many tools we purchase in our high-tech age have special features that make them useful for a variety of applications or functions. Sometimes those features aren't obvious by looking at the tool's exterior. So we have to take a close look, examine all the buttons and dials, and learn what they're for. Yes, we even have to read the instruction manual, as tedious as that may be.

Although you have probably never thought of Sunday School curriculum in high-tech terms, the resources that get dropped into your lap every quarter also have many features that bear taking a closer look. Maybe you haven't thought about some of them; you've just become familiar with the curriculum and are comfortable with your own way of developing a lesson plan. That's okay. However, thoroughly understanding the tools you have can make a big difference in effectively using them in class. So even if you're quite familiar with the materials, let's take a close look inside and get acquainted with the essential elements so you know what they are and why they are there.

First Impression

First impressions are important—even long lasting. So let's start with the cover. A quick glance at the cover of any teacher guide will tell you which three-month (thirteen-lesson) quarter the material is intended for (fall, winter, spring, or summer), the age or grade level(s), and often the theme(s) being presented. The cover illustration or photography may correlate with the quarter's content, spotlight the students at the given age level, or simply provide a colorful design.

Looking Inside

Resource Information

Before rushing into the "meat" of the quarter's studies, take a peek at the inside front cover. There you generally will find information about the various curriculum resources available for that age level or other resources that may supplement the Christian education and discipleship program of your church. Perhaps you have not had opportunity to use some of these items. You can check the website information given to find out more about those products or call the toll-free number provided.

Publisher and Staff

Then, on the first page, you will find publisher and staff information. While the names may not be familiar to you, you

can be assured they represent qualified people who are com-
mitted to providing solid, Spirit-filled lessons for your students.
Some names appear regularly in the writer list.

Units of Study

You also will see an overview of the quarter's contents. In most
cases the studies are divided into two or three units, with three to
seven studies per unit. While some themes lend themselves to
several lessons, others can be covered in three or four. Breaking
down a quarter into two or three units is helpful in two ways.
(1) Units offer a variety for both the teacher and student.
Including an assortment of studies provides a mental break and
helps prevent belaboring a theme. (2) Units broaden the scope of
themes that can be covered in each level of curriculum. In some
cases there will be a shift from Old Testament to New Testament
or a mix of issue-related topics.

Informing students when unit themes are changing can be
helpful, especially if the shift is from a Bible topic (book study) to
a contemporary issue. For example, one quarter in the Preteen
level was divided into units about God's laws (four studies),
attitudes (four studies), and highlights on the Book of Revelation
(five studies). If students are notified a week in advance about a
shift in unit themes, the change is not as abrupt.

Each unit is preceded by a unit introduction that gives a
helpful overview of the unit's contents and often provides suggestions for special activities that will help reinforce the lessons
to be presented. Also, the resource packet often includes unit
posters that can be displayed in the classroom. You can display
all posters at the beginning of the quarter and give a brief
overview of each or display them the week prior to the shift in
themes. Sharing this overview with the students the week prior
to a unit shift can help make the transition smoother.

In some cases, depending on the quarter's overall emphasis,
the units will be developed along the same basic topic or

theme. For example, a quarter of Primary lessons was divided into three units that all dealt with stories about Peter and his friends—"Peter Follows Jesus," "Peter Needs Forgiveness," and "Peter Leads the First Church."

Guiding Elements

How-to information. Additional information found in the front of the teacher guide focuses on the guide's various features, helping you understand how it is put together. Also, information is given about the supplementary items, including the resource packet and student books. Reviewing this segment will acquaint you with the elements of the lesson structure and how the supplementary items correlate with the studies presented.

Curriculum philosophies. In the leader guide materials is information about the philosophy behind the educational or instructional design of the curriculum you are using. Toddlers and Twos through Preschool, Kindergarten through Preteen, and Youth through Adult curricula are developed according to a particular learning theory that accommodates the age-level characteristics and the kinds of educational approaches that will work best for those levels along with an applied knowledge of the learning styles within those levels.

Here is an overview of the philosophies on which Radiant Life curriculum is built:

Toddlers and Twos Through Preschool
GUIDED PLAY/GUIDED LEARNING

Important Issues
• Curriculum is based on measurable objectives.
• Moral development objectives guide the life application emphases.
• Learning centers are used to provide a high level of activity, practice in biblical living, and variety for developing minds and bodies.

- Intentional questions are inserted to help keep children focused on the emphasis for a given lesson.
- A wide variety of storytelling methods is utilized.
- Teachable moments arise when children are engaged in various activities that focus on essential elements and applications of the lessons.

Philosophies
- Curriculum is based on an established scope and sequence.
- Students learn through purposeful play.
- Teachers are responsible for monitoring the students' teachable moments.
- Teachers are encouraged to listen carefully for cues that indicate children are picking up on key elements in the lessons taught.
- Objectives are stated simply.
- Bible stories are centered on foundational, well-known Bible accounts.
- Intentional questions are written into the curriculum and are the cornerstone of the learning process.

Kindergarten Through Preteen
ACTIVE LEARNING LESSON CYCLE

Important Issues
- Curriculum is based on measurable objectives.
- Moral development objectives guide the life application emphases.
- Objectives are spiraled, indicating that as themes are revisited throughout the scope and sequence, the lessons are presented from different perspectives.
- Prior knowledge is considered. Teachers determine how much students already know about the lesson and review what they have learned in the previous lesson.

- An introductory overview is provided regarding what will be shared in each lesson. "In this week's lesson, we will . . ." This establishes the lesson's focus.
- Explanation includes communicating the Bible lesson content along with guided practice (activities) that engage the students in the learning process.
- Application involves activities that reinforce the lesson content as well as character development issues.
- A "taking it with me" segment provides exercises that will help students internalize concepts and truths as well as make specific application in their daily lives. This also involves review of concepts learned.

Philosophies
- Curriculum is built on an established scope and sequence.
- Students learn in a variety of ways.
- Information is introduced, and students are encouraged to interact with the material (cognitively and/or physically) through various activities.
- The teacher checks for understanding throughout the lesson.
- Measurable objectives and moral development objectives guide the lesson.
- Objectives and questions are spiraled to help students move toward higher levels of thinking about the subject matter presented.
- Learning-styles theory guides the writing and teacher's choice of activities. Activities are intentionally included to accommodate auditory, visual, tactual, and kinesthetic learners.
- The lesson plan is written for "skim," "scan," "information seeking," and ease of reading. Major points stand out for teachers to quickly skim through the general outline of the lesson, both in preparation and presentation. Subpoints and boldface highlights are used to help teachers scan important details. Content is "chunked" in blocks of activities,

commentary, applicational emphases, and so on to present important information and organize the lesson presentation. Appropriate readability levels are developed for both teachers and students.

Youth Through Adult
INTERACTIVE LEARNING

Important Issues
- Curriculum is based on measurable objectives.
- Moral development objectives guide the applicational emphases.
- Introductory activities/information are presented for each lesson.
- Bible content involves lecture along with a variety of questions, case studies, group activities, etc.
- Application and "taking it with me" emphases are provided.

Philosophies
- Curriculum is built on an established scope and sequence.
- Interactive learning guides much of the lesson presentation.
- Intentional questions, small-group interactions, case studies, hypothetical situations, and the like reinforce and explain concepts.
- Bible study is the core of the curriculum.
- Application is an important aspect of the learning.
- Student "life experience" affects the course of the lesson.
- Lesson plan is written for "skim," "scan," "information seeking," and ease of reading (see explanations under Kindergarten through Preteen philosophies).

Teacher Training
"In-service training" is a vital component of Radiant Life curriculum. Even if you have been teaching for thirty years or more, most likely you are still open to fresh insights on the age level you are teaching and ways to communicate more effectively.

Teacher training is another vital element incorporated in each teacher guide. Teacher Skill Builder articles deal with such topics as discussion activities, personal performance evaluation, student involvement in the learning process, alternatives in student groupings, ideas for motivating students to learn, and more. Information on effective lesson planning is included regularly in most teacher guides. Also, helpful guidelines on leading a child or youth to Christ and leading students into the baptism in the Holy Spirit are included across the age-level spectrum. These teaching elements will help you sharpen your skills in the classroom and develop a sense of effective ministry.

What's Next?

"Coming Next Quarter" information is usually featured in the front matter of the teacher guide or on the back cover. This gives you a heads-up on future unit themes and topics.

Lesson Content—Introductory Elements

Bible Text

At the top of the first page for each lesson is the unit theme, date, and lesson title or topic. Following that is the Bible text from which the lesson is drawn. Bible text coverage will vary according to the age level and general direction of the study. In children's curriculum, the Bible text provides the backdrop for the lesson. In some Youth and many Adult studies, the Bible text will be closely exposited. In either case, in a Bible-centered curriculum, the Bible text provides the platform on which everything else is built.

Teachers sometimes are uncertain about which Bible version they should use in lesson preparation and presentation. The two versions most commonly cited in Radiant Life Resources are the King James Version and the New International Version. Early Childhood and Early Elementary curriculums also make use of the New Century Version. These choices reflect an effort to provide options as well as helping students understand God's Word in today's language. Writers will sometimes incorporate a variety of versions for the sake of comparison and further clarification of Scripture passages. This is particularly true of Youth and Adult resources.

Lesson Objective

Closely connected to the Bible text is the objective. This is the target you're aiming for with the lesson. Everything done prior to, during, and after the lesson presentation supports or reinforces the objective statement. For example, in a Preschool lesson about Paul encouraging others in the midst of a shipwreck recorded in Acts 27, the objective is: "To help the child explain that Paul encouraged people who were afraid." The objective generally targets specific information (Bible knowledge) the students should acquire in the lesson presentation.

Life Application Objective

Life application is vital to the Christian education/discipleship process. Thus, arising out of the objective is a crucial life application emphasis in each lesson. Sometimes conveyed in a brief statement or just a single word, the life application emphasis centers on a core value or moral guideline for the lesson. This is the affective dimension of the study. Effort is made not only to enable students to understand God's Word, but to help them apply it to life and thereby build moral character as well. Why is this so important? Children, youth, and adults are being influenced daily by a postmodern culture that neither accepts or adheres to the biblical, moral principles and absolutes that believers in Christ understand as givens. Principles of integrity, trust, honesty, fairness, righteousness, and others often are being redefined by a society that desires to make everything relative and conditional. Therefore, in conjunction with the unchanging truth of God's Word, students need to recognize that moral laws are unchanging as well. Not only must they know these laws intellectually; more important, they need to understand how to apply them practically in daily living. The life application emphasis is designed to convey one significant moral value, principle, or guideline the students will remember and apply.

In a Preteen Christmas lesson about the birth of Christ, the objective states: "To help the students discover that Jesus' birth was very carefully planned by God." The life application emphasis states: "Reverence: To teach the students to celebrate Christmas with new reverence for God's Son." In a society that commercializes Christmas, students will learn the significance of Christ's birth from a biblical and historical perspective and, in doing so, will gain a greater appreciation of and reverence for Jesus Christ, God's Son.

Life application relates closely to the issue of moral development. Children, youth, and adults move through various stages of moral development as they mature in their understanding of social and cultural norms as well as biblical principles for living. An important part of Christian education is to help students progress to higher levels of moral development.

Unfortunately, many students, even adults, primarily operate on very basic levels of moral development. For example, they may do the right thing only so they won't get caught or for what they can get out of it (What's in it for me?). Students of all ages need to progress to higher levels of moral development. Ultimately, we want to help them make a choice or decision that is based on more than fear of punishment, the possibility of reward, or respect for a set of rules established by society; we want to help them make that choice because it simply is the right thing to do.

The spiritual dynamics of salvation through faith in Jesus Christ and the empowerment of the Holy Spirit enable a believer to advance more readily to higher levels of moral development. Progress is not dependent entirely on human effort or sheer determination to improve one's character; instead, a renewing of the mind and a transformation of character take place as the believer aligns his or her life according to God's will and purpose.

Key Verse

A vital ingredient to building our base of spiritual understanding is hiding God's Word in our hearts. Thus each study also presents a key verse, a Bible verse selected to represent the thrust of the study. In most cases students are encouraged to memorize these verses to further expand their Bible knowledge. Activities are provided in the curriculum to help reinforce learning. The biblical mandate to hide God's Word in our hearts is an important guideline in a Bible-centered curriculum. Key verses are presented in both the King James Version and the New International Version and, in some cases, the New Century Version.

Fundamental Truths

Many studies throughout the scope and sequence touch on fundamental truths or doctrinal statements of the Church. Therefore, often you will see a "We Believe" segment included on the beginning page of the lesson. This highlights the doctrinal truth being taught. For example, in a Primary lesson that presents the story of the angel's message to Joseph prior to Jesus' birth, the "We Believe" statement reads: "Jesus' birth was unlike any other birth. He was born of a virgin. All other babies have human fathers. Jesus, the one and only Son of God, had no earthly father." This statement alerts the teacher that a key doctrine regarding the virgin birth of Jesus is being presented.

Teacher Focus

Prior to the lesson presentation, a "Teacher Focus" segment gives you a bird's-eye view of the lesson. It sometimes is written in a devotional style or in a way that provides a special insight that will help you focus the study on the students' needs. For example, a teacher focus presented in a Kindergarten study titled "Good News for Zechariah" relates God's promise through an angel that Zechariah's wife, Elizabeth, would have a son named John who would one day announce Jesus to the world. The focus is on helping each child trust God to keep His promises.

The teacher focus reads:

> The dictionary defines a promise as "a declaration assuring that one will or will not do something." People sometimes fail to keep promises because they forget or because they lack resources. But God never forgets, and He never runs out of resources. God always keeps His promises.

> As you prepare this lesson, think about times you have seen God keep His promises. Praise God for those kept promises. Then help your students understand that they too can trust God.

The teacher focus helps set the tone for the lesson and encourages teachers to consider God's work in their lives and convey that truth more powerfully to the students.

Checklist

In Preschool through Preteen curriculum, you will find a checklist of items needed for that lesson. The checklist is arranged according to the major subheads in the lesson plan. Additionally, a suggested time frame for each subhead is indicated. Since the amount of class time varies from place to place, teachers will need to decide how much time can be spent on any given segment or activity within that segment. Class times projections range from forty to sixty minutes.

Lesson Presentation

Lesson Lead-In

Lesson lead-in content varies somewhat in the Early Childhood through Upper Elementary materials. As children arrive for class, welcoming activities help pull them into the group and prepare them for the coming lesson. Activities may include singing songs and reviewing the key verse for the lesson. Older children are engaged in lesson review activities. In some cases skits or music from resource packet CDs are played to set the stage for the coming Bible lesson.

Lecture, discussion, and interaction balance lesson presentations throughout the curriculum spectrum. At some levels a basic overview of the lesson content is complemented by a variety of activities that help convey and/or reinforce the Bible lesson. Although the lesson content is written in a way that can be read to the students, teachers are encouraged to carefully review the lesson and then present it in their own words.

Learning Activities

Activities interspersed throughout the body of the lesson include student book items, resource packet materials, and other suggested activities. These represent options that the teacher can incorporate depending on facilities, resources, the amount of class time available, and the number of students. A variety of options allow the teacher to use something that will fit almost any class situation.

But why are so many activities included? Isn't it important just to convey what the Bible teaches? Certainly the focus must remain on what God's Word teaches us, but activities help cement key truths and facts that are important for our understanding and spiritual growth. Activities that engage the students in the learning process also make learning enjoyable.

Let's suppose you're examining cake mixes in the grocery store and you notice a major-brand mix and a generic mix placed side by side. You see that the generic mix is significantly less expensive than the major brand. However, as you review the major brand, you see a full-color picture of a finished product that looks good enough to eat right off the box. When you look at the generic package, the graphics aren't nearly as appealing. Producers of the major brand are willing to spend many thousands, if not millions, of dollars more to put a full-color picture on their box because they know that it will capture interest.

Bible truth is the most important thing we can share. It is life changing. Sadly, God's truths sometimes are presented in less than appealing ways. Using student-involvement activities in Sunday School is like putting a colorful wrapping around your lesson presentation. They make learning fun, appealing, and memorable.

Studies show us the following about learning retention.

People generally remember:
10% of what they read
20% of what they hear
30% of what they see
50% of what they hear and see
70% of what they say and write
90% of what they say as they do a thing

Clearly, much more information is retained as students are involved in learning reinforcement activities.

Both the Young Teen and High School curricula involve a significant amount of student interaction along with Bible commentary and lecture material. The *Connections* Adult curriculum also presents a strong emphasis on discussion. Designed to accommodate adult Bible fellowship format, *Connections* is structured around a teacher-as-facilitator model. Instead of lecture with some discussion, the facilitator presents an overview of the study, then involves the students in small-group discussion. Then, the facilitator calls for responses from the groups and ties together or synthesizes the thrust of the discussion in accord with the study aim or character focus. *Connections* can also be used in a more traditional lecture/discussion format.

The standard Adult curriculum is structured for more of a lecture/discussion model of teaching. However, students can be engaged in a number of discussion opportunities.

Life Application

Life application is a major component in the teaching-learning process. Every lesson plan in Radiant Life Resources presents this vital emphasis tied directly to the "Life Application" focus for the study. Students are helped to understand how the study affects their lives and what they should do in response to the study. In many cases students are encouraged to do something during the week following the lesson to intentionally apply what they have learned. Teachers can inquire as to whether students have done those things during the week, thus providing an indicator of movement toward discipleship and growth in spiritual maturity.

An important life application emphasis is evangelism response. The Sunday School class provides a fertile opportunity for children, youth, and adults to consider their need of Christ. Also, a number of studies throughout the scope and sequence encourage students to seek the baptism in the Holy Spirit. Guidelines for both salvation and baptism in the Holy Spirit are provided regularly in the teacher guides. These must never be viewed only as fillers or items tacked onto the lessons. They are vital to the spiritual dynamic of the teaching-learning process.

Student Resources

A number of student resources are provided across the Radiant Life Resources spectrum. These include student lesson guides, workbooks, handwork packets, and story papers. Weekly lesson plans indicate where, when, and how these items are to be incorporated. In most cases the student guides and workbooks contain items to be done at some point during or after the lesson presentations. Though they can be viewed as options along with other activities, the printed materials are generally presented as primary suggestions. They are designed to integrally relate to the points being made in the studies.

Take-home story papers are provided from Early Childhood through Upper Elementary. A story paper is also provided for the Adult level. In some cases there are direct or indirect tie-ins with the weekly lessons, either through the stories presented or the activities. Parents are encouraged to read stories to children in the Early Childhood years. A major purpose of these resources is to help relate Christian living to everyday life.

Resource Packets

Each level of curriculum provides a resource packet containing a variety of items from posters, charts, and maps to work sheets, overhead masters, and CDs. Visual aid sheets at the Early Childhood and Early Elementary levels are also available to help illustrate the lessons. Items contained in these resources are referenced within the teaching plans. Lesson presentations are greatly augmented by using these creative resources. Use of these items along with the student books will enhance learning, making it more enjoyable for you and your students.

How Can I Make It Fit?
Adapting Curriculum to Your Sunday School Program

No doubt you've seen one advertised on TV—a kitchen gadget that can cut, slice, dice, and seemingly do almost anything. No home should be without one; and for the incredibly low price of $19.99, you can have your own. Yet despite any tool's marvels, it can't be everything to every situation.

Similarly, if you're looking for a Sunday School curriculum that exactly fits every teacher, every student, every situation, every church, you won't find that either. There are no one-size-fits-all curricula on the market. Some adaptation is needed regardless of how innovative the materials are. However, Radiant Life curriculum can be adjusted to fit a wide spectrum of needs or settings in a church relative to size, number of students, learning styles, facilities, and budget. This chapter explores some ways that Radiant Life curriculum can be adapted to a variety of situations.

Student Groupings

Most important in deciding the best use of curriculum in the local church is the number of students attending and whether they are grouped according to age or grade. Babies and toddlers to two-year-olds vary greatly in their ability to comprehend material that is taught. That is why Radiant Life provides distinctly different resources for those age levels. As the children progress in age, it is advantageous to group them by their grade level whenever possible—a class for first graders, another for second graders, and so on. However, that is not feasible in every situation.

Class Divisions

For example, a church of fewer than one hundred in total attendance may have five primary age children, two middlers, and six preteens. In that case it may be best to have a class for primaries and group the middlers with the preteens. While there are differences in age-level characteristics between middlers and preteens, the teaching plan can be adjusted to accommodate the younger children. In most cases where there are not enough students to justify use of another classroom and engaging an additional teacher, the students should be grouped to the next higher age level. While the situation just described could be adjusted the other way (if there were fewer preteens than middlers), the older children may become disenchanted with the curriculum designed for the younger age level.

Care should be taken, however, not to group too broadly. For example, if there are only two first graders and several third-through sixth-grade children, it would not be advisable to merge the primaries with the middlers. The gap between first and third graders is significant, particularly with regard to reading levels and attention span. The developmental gap between third graders and fifth graders is significant also; however, reading ability and attention span issues will not be as marked.

As age and grade levels increase, grouping issues become less difficult. Young teen and high school classes can be merged without a great deal of difficulty. However, at those levels, topics and themes are carefully chosen to track with the emotional, relational, and spiritual needs of teenagers. Adults generally can be grouped together regardless of age; however, the interests of young adults will be piqued by resources that encourage interaction and discussion. Therefore, using an alternate Adult curriculum like *Connections* may be advisable for young adults.

When ordering classroom materials for school-age students and up, it is helpful to provide at least two additional copies of student guides, workbooks, and story papers. This will accommodate visitors and new members who become part of the Sunday School class.

Teacher Availability and Experience

While age groupings are very important to class arrangements and curriculum usage, the availability of teachers is also an important factor. Small or growing churches may not have enough teachers to fill closely graded class groupings. In such cases the best approach, again, is to group students according to the next grade level until additional teachers can be appointed.

Training and experience are also significant factors in beginning new Sunday School classes and using Radiant Life curriculum. Although your church may not require that you enroll in specified training classes, being involved in training sessions can be very beneficial to you personally and to the overall effectiveness of your Christian education program. A number of very helpful teacher training materials are available through the national Sunday School Department at the General Council of the Assemblies of God in Springfield, Missouri. These resources can be tailored to fit various time segments and group settings. Those resources together with this training course can be tremendously helpful to you by providing guidance in the use of curricular materials, lesson planning, age-level characteristics, learning styles, and more. Training in these areas will help you not only to understand the practical aspects of teaching, but also to realize that the task is doable and that the resources available to you are teacher and student friendly.

Training helps also are available in every teacher's guide. "Teacher Skill Builder" articles convey important information on a wide variety of subjects. You are encouraged to remove and file these articles for future reference. Additional helps are available through Radiant Life's website <www.radiantlife.org>. Check this site periodically for a variety of training articles as well as information on acquiring numerous training resources developed by the national Sunday School Department.

While you may have many years of teaching experience, you always will benefit greatly from Radiant Life curriculum resources; however, the curriculum should never be viewed as a straitjacket. Knowledge of your individual students, their learning styles, the type of content being presented, and other factors will aid you in making creative adjustments in the presentation of the weekly lessons. Rather than stifle creativity by demanding that a specified outline or process be followed each week, Radiant Life offers a flexible teaching plan that enables teachers to incorporate their own insights and activities. Curriculum must always be viewed as a guide, a springboard for topics and themes that will help students of all ages better understand God's Word and its application to life.

If you are less experienced, you will be helped by the carefully selected topics and lesson plans. Student book and resource packet items can be used as flexibly as experience and class schedules allow. Seasoned teachers also will benefit from these things and use them as foundations for building carefully tailored lesson presentations.

Levels of Student Knowledge

In virtually every class situation, you will encounter students with varying degrees of Bible knowledge. While one student may not be able to tell you whether Leviticus is in the Old or New Testament, another will be able to find even the most obscure passages in just seconds. One will rattle off the details of a story before you have a chance to tell it, while another will be hearing it for the first time.

For those who lack basic Bible knowledge, the solution is fairly simple: Go over the points carefully. But what should you do when you have students who are particularly sharp and have all the answers?

- Engage them in the presentation by asking questions that will challenge their knowledge of the Bible story or its application.
- Involve them in role-play or story acting. Early and upper elementary children particularly enjoy this. Young teens and high school students will enjoy role-play situations that deal with life-related issues.
- Assign them something to research during the week that will shed light on the study.
- Allow a student to relate the events of the story in his or her own words, or have more than one student contribute various details.
- Focus on the various activities suggested in the curriculum, whether work sheets, crafts, or student book and resource packet items.

Remember that you're teaching all the time, not only when you're talking, and students are not necessarily learning if they're sitting still. Students learn much more when they are involved in the learning process. Experiment with adapting the curriculum to fit the needs of students who are well versed and need to be challenged.

In some cases, particularly in churches which have many new converts, the level of Bible knowledge will be limited. Whether your students have a little or a lot of Bible knowledge, these levels will in some way affect the use of curriculum resources.

Upper Elementary Through Adult

Levels of Bible knowledge will be more apparent in the Upper Elementary through Adult classes. Formerly nonchurched children, youth, and adults will have little if any familiarity with even the most basic Bible stories. Attending church itself is a new experience for them. Teachers need to be prepared to adjust their lesson presentations accordingly. You may need to spend some class time bringing students along who have no concept of the basics. As the regular lessons are presented, some additional explanations may be necessary. However, care needs to be taken not to lose the attention of those who are familiar with the basics. Students who are well versed in basic Bible knowledge can help explain these things to students who are new to the church. In that way, the more knowledgeable students are given opportunity to reinforce what they already know plus be a blessing to others who need additional information.

Students, particularly in the early elementary through teen years, can be encouraged to work together on some of the student book or discussion activities. This eliminates having some children struggle with activities while others work through them with ease. Not only will this help newer students grasp the information, but also the teaching plan will be expedited by your not having to wait for some students to complete exercises before moving on with the lesson.

Limited Church Background

If the corresponding grade-level curriculum is used with students with little or no church background, care must be taken to proceed slowly. Some lessons may require more than one session while others may be bypassed in order to convey basic truths. For example, if a quarter is divided into units on the Bible, the

Minor Prophets, and spiritual warfare, it may be best to spend more time on the Bible and spiritual warfare units and bypass the Minor Prophets. The Minor Prophets can be dealt with at a later time when basic Bible knowledge is established. If you do choose to omit a unit, the more knowledgeable students should be apprised of the reason. Again, it will be very important to engage them in the teaching process.

Spending more time on given themes can apply to students well versed in the Bible as well. If interest in a theme is strong, you may find value in giving more time to that theme instead of moving on with the prescribed units.

The curriculum development process is not based on arbitrary decisions to complete a thematic "quota." Careful and prayerful attention is given to planning the scope and sequence across the entire spectrum. A balanced treatment of topics and themes is carefully structured. Bible book studies, doctrinal and theological themes, as well as contemporary topics are woven into the development plan. However, since every teaching situation is different, the issue of flexibility comes into focus. That is when the teacher must rely on personal knowledge of the students and the guidance of the Holy Spirit in planning lesson presentations.

The Teen and Bible Knowledge

Teens from nonchurched families may be affected more dramatically than younger students by a lack of Bible knowledge. If they are in a group of peers who are familiar with biblical and doctrinal issues, their lack of understanding may be a source of embarrassment, discouragement, or confusion. Care must be taken to avoid placing them in awkward situations, such as looking up Bible passages or answering questions that require basic Bible knowledge to answer. Since it would likely be awkward to use a lower grade-level curriculum with teens who thrive on peer acceptance, patience, sensitivity, and understanding are essential.

67

Student Interest or Need

Just as students vary in levels of Bible knowledge and understanding, they vary in levels of interest in certain topics and themes. Whether you are experienced or just beginning, reliance on the Holy Spirit is vital to your lesson preparation and presentation. Depending on the needs of individual students, the Spirit may direct you toward an emphasis that expands upon the printed material for a given lesson. Certainly no writer, editor, or publisher can know the specific needs of every student or class. Reliance on the Holy Spirit's sovereign leadership must, above all else, be supreme in the Christian education of children, youth, and adults.

Crisis Events

Sometimes current events locally, nationally, or globally will dictate the need for a unique emphasis in the class session. It is certainly your prerogative to deal with those things if you sense they are of great consequence to your students. In times of crisis, a direction other than that presented in the printed curriculum may need to be taken. In such eventualities, teachers are also encouraged to consult the Radiant Life website, particularly in the case of national or global crises. Effort will be made to provide biblical guidance on such matters that can be conveyed in the classroom. In any event, awareness of current events is vital to helping students understand how the Christian worldview applies to real-life circumstances.

Special Interests

At times students will be particularly interested in or fascinated by a topic being presented. This is sometimes true with themes that touch on the end times or the supernatural. When interest is piqued, you may want to deal at greater length on the topic rather than move on to the next lesson. Of course, care must be taken to avoid going well beyond what either the Word of God or curricular materials present. Speculation on some matters only leads to confusion and misinformation. Again, sensitivity both to the leading of the Holy Spirit and to student interest is vital.

Learning Styles

Learning styles, particularly among children, influence how curriculum is used in class. For example, auditory learners relate most to storytelling, kinesthetic learners need to have opportunity to move around, and tactual learners need hands-on involvement with the lesson. As lessons are developed, it is important to review the kinds of presentations and activities that will best engage the students.

Knowing the children is absolutely essential to adjusting the presentation and using the curriculum effectively with various kinds of learners. If only one approach (lecture, for example) is used, some or several of the children may tune out or become sources of continual disciplinary problems.

Radiant Life curriculum is developed with various kinds of learners in mind. Almost every lesson has activities to accommodate the different learning styles of children. It would be difficult to address all learning styles every week, but intentional efforts to plan lessons with those in mind will make the learning experience much more effective for both student and teacher. (See chapter 5 for in-depth information on learning styles.)

Cultural and Ethnic Backgrounds

While Bible stories are timeless and the characters presented are predominantly of Middle Eastern ethnicity, the ethnic background of the Sunday School class can influence the application of truths and principles learned in Scripture. Though many illustrations will apply to people of any culture and context, the teacher must keep certain cultural nuances in focus to avoid being offensive or irrelevant. Great care is given in the curriculum development process to avoid casting a particular ethnic group in a bad light or conveying negative stereotypes.

Students of ethnic and cultural backgrounds wrestle with many of the same kinds of situations and problems. For example, an anecdote that presents a preteen student deciding whether to cheat on a test can relate to any cultural or ethnic background, from middle-class suburbia to the inner city. While the curriculum may present various situations students can find themselves in, the life application emphases can be adjusted to fit those situations.

The printed story is a springboard for other possible directions. Do not regard what is in print as the only option. Obviously, no curriculum can accommodate the full spectrum of cultural and ethnic backgrounds. Again, teachers must be sensitive to their students and craft or modify illustrations and applications to fit their classes.

Care is taken in Radiant Life Resources also to reflect various cultural and ethnic backgrounds in visual illustrations. This is particularly true of posters that illustrate contemporary characters. Effort is made to include Hispanic, African American, and Asian characters as well as other ethnic groupings.

Fitting lessons and applications to the cultural context becomes increasingly important as more churches are planted in the inner cities and among ethnic groups. Teachers who find themselves in settings with strong ethnic representations and cultural backgrounds do well to review in advance the various life application emphases throughout a given quarter of studies and spotlight areas that may need to be adjusted for their contexts. Doing so will eliminate last-minute dilemmas about determining how stories can be adjusted to fit or trying to recreate appropriate emphases.

Class Schedule

Perhaps nothing challenges teachers more than trying to fit everything within the prescribed class time. Schedules vary from thirty minutes to two hours, with most falling within a forty- to forty-five-minute time frame. Virtually every lesson contains more information and activities than can be used within that period of time.

The key is advance planning, taking time to study and review the material well ahead of time, keeping in mind the amount of class time available. Lesson content in Radiant Life Resources curriculum is streamlined and flexible, with a focused, single objective. Enough information is provided in the Bible lesson segment to provide a good understanding of the theme being presented, yet it is flexible enough to be condensed or expanded. If the class schedule allows one hour, more time can be spent looking up and reading Scripture passages, discussing questions, doing activities, and so on. If only thirty minutes are available, decisions must be made as to the most salient information.

Teachers often struggle with trying to fit in activity suggestions while still allowing time to convey the lesson and have discussion. Some even feel guilty if they do not squeeze everything into the printed lesson plan. Remember, not everything in the printed lesson has to be accomplished to teach successfully or thoroughly. Picking and choosing what to teach and what to have students do in any given session is the teacher's prerogative. Depending on the topic, a limited schedule may demand spending more time on the actual Bible study; in other instances, the students may benefit more by being involved in various activities that relate to the Bible context, especially if it is a familiar account. Again, knowing the students, the material, and the schedule are vital. Trusting the Holy Spirit's guidance also is essential.

Using Student Books and Resource Items

A wide variety of student books and resource items are available for each level of Radiant Life Resources curriculum. These are the backbone of the curriculum structure, providing lesson-related stories and activities that engage the students directly in the learning process.

At the Early Childhood level, student-directed items in the resource packets are used heavily in the teaching process. Little children learn a great deal through guided play. Using board books, puppets, and other manipulative items with babies and toddlers helps capture attention and convey meaningful information. As children progress into their preschool years, more time can be spent with stories and songs, although involving them in guided play activities is still important. Not everything in the student books or resource items has to be used every time. Few class schedules will allow that. Therefore, teachers need to pick and choose what they will be able to fit into their designated class time and lesson plan.

Variety

Variety is a vital dynamic in classroom teaching. Using the same approach every time will get monotonous and predictable for both the teacher and students. Therefore, plan to use the student materials and resource items in a variety of ways. At times this will mean incorporating those items precisely when they are called for in the teacher guide. At other times it will mean having the students work through the activities after the lesson presentation as reinforcement. Or it may mean sending some items home with the students to work on at their leisure. In any case, there is not necessarily only one way to use the items, or even a right way. Their use can be adapted to fit schedules, teaching and learning styles, and facilities.

Learning Differently

When student guide activities are used in class, teachers need to be sensitive to varying levels of accomplishment, particularly in the elementary grades. Some children will be able to work puzzles and codes very quickly, while others will struggle. What often happens is that when a faster student completes the work, he or she will blurt out the answers, making it pointless for those still finishing to continue. If there are some students who are especially fast at solving complex activities, consider letting them help or work with those who are not as fast. That way all will feel a sense of accomplishment and teamwork. Also, partnering children in these activities can help break down cliques that often exclude children who are a little slower in their work.

In some cases, depending on the activity, children can be instructed to work on certain parts instead of completing the entire activity. If those who do not complete work as quickly are given segments that will be focused on later, they may have opportunity to get their work finished before being called on.

Timing

Sometimes activities that clearly will take several minutes to complete may best be left to the end of the session for completion as time permits. Or those activities can be sent home with the children to finish on their own. Waiting for everyone to finish can be frustrating for the teacher who wants to move on with presentation. A good practice during the lesson preparation time is for the teacher to work through the activities personally. Though the teacher may be able to do them more quickly than the students, he or she will have a gauge for predicting how much time each activity will take.

Choices

As a rule the printed resources that are purchased for the classroom are suggested as the primary activities. That stands to reason since the church has invested financially in those materials. The writers, editors, and designers of the Radiant Life curriculum invest a great deal of time and creative energy to develop creative and meaningful resources. Though not indispensable to the teaching-learning process, these resources are presented as priority choices in the lesson plan. Other activity suggestions are usually listed secondarily, though not necessarily of less significance or relevance to the lesson. Again, as teachers prepare their lessons with their schedules, students, and facilities in mind, they must make decisions regarding the best use of the resources provided.

Lots of Extras

In addition to the student books, a number of innovative tools can be found in the resource packets. These include posters, Bible character visuals, maps, time lines, student work sheets, songs, CD recordings, and more. In most cases the packet items serve to convey important points of information visually, audibly, or through direct student interaction. Visual aids and posters are particularly important to children. These help them better understand the actual events and characters mentioned in the Bible lessons. A good rule of thumb is to mount visuals on the classroom walls as they are used. Not only does this add color and interest to the classroom, but also it continues to reinforce the lessons learned.

Activity sheets are designed to be duplicated for the students. These generally involve skits, case studies, and other interactive items that engage the students directly in the lessons. Other sheets may include information on historical or cultural backgrounds to lessons or other materials that add perspective and dimension. These can be used effectively for student reports.

In higher levels, particularly in the Adult curricula, overhead transparency masters are included. In many cases these convey outline points, quotes, or other salient pieces of information to be presented at various places in the lesson. If overhead projectors are not used, the content can be used in PowerPoint presentations. Or the masters can be duplicated as handouts or information sheets and distributed to the students.

As a Sunday School teacher, you will continually face the challenge of adapting the resources to fit your local situation. You know your students better than anyone else. You know their backgrounds, interests, and needs. As you develop personal relationships, you will gain even more knowledge that will help guide you in your lesson preparation and presentation. Use that knowledge and understanding, together with sensitivity to the Holy Spirit's leading, to help you make the best use of the resources you have.

Letting Them Learn:
A Basic Guide to Understanding Learning Styles
by Sandy Friesen

The teacher's role in the development of children has been passionately debated over the years. Some have said that children are born without personalities or learning preferences, and that it is up to parents and teachers to create a child's personality. Others argue that children are born with a set personality and learning style, and therefore parents and teachers should step aside and let nature take its course. But as in most issues, the truth probably rests somewhere between the extremes. For the purpose of this chapter, I make the following assumption: Children are probably born with *temperament tendencies, learning styles,* and *personality preferences*. Parents and teachers are responsible to guide, direct, and help children fulfill Christ's commission to love God and love others as themselves.

Where does the teacher begin in the process of developing the child? Historically, "to train a child" meant that the process was emphasized and the child was adapted to the process. In recent years education has undergone a paradigm shift; that is, teachers have begun to think about "training" differently. This new paradigm emphasizes the concept of understanding the individual child. There are many dimensions to fulfilling that concept. Four easy-to-remember guidelines are listed below and expanded upon in this chapter:

Discover who the child is.

Develop a flexible plan to "grow" a healthy child.

Determine to meet the child's needs by understanding your own strategies.

Demonstrate a wide range of strategies to meet the child's needs.

Discover Who the Child Is

Individuals have a tendency toward a certain temperament from birth. Longitudinal studies have found that individuals monitored from infancy into adulthood change very little from their initial reaction to the world. Babies were described in one of four ways: (1) easy, (2) slow-to-warm-up, (3) difficult (challenging), and (4) a mix.

Easy children (approximately 40 percent) were those who reacted positively to new stimuli. These children were curious and unafraid of new objects, pictures, or situations. They cooed, smiled, or responded with excitement when placed in an unknown situation.

Slow-to-warm-up children (approximately 15 percent) faced new objects or situations with trepidation. They were usually cautious at first, warming up to the "new" slowly and deliberately. They sometimes cried and refused to deal with the unknown, but with careful and supportive coaxing, they accepted the situation.

Challenging children (approximately 10 percent) tended to find the "new" overwhelming and were disgruntled with being asked to entertain the concept of a new situation. These infants, children, and adults took a great deal of convincing and support to accept anything outside the routine. The first reaction to a change was a resounding "No!" Parents and caretakers spent a great deal of time transitioning these children into being comfortable with new people, objects, or situations.

Mix children (approximately 35 percent) were unpredictable. They could respond in any of the above manners.

Individuals develop learning preferences that stay relatively constant throughout their lives. We call this their "learning style." Several learning style models are relevant to the development and teaching of children. We will briefly examine Rita and Kenneth Dunn's model. They have researched how children learn with some exciting results. According to their findings, children have preferences (much like being right-handed or left-handed) that they favor throughout their lives.

The Dunns examined the environmental, emotional, sociological, physiological, and psychological needs of individual children. Each area was subdivided to include elements that affected the children. For example, in the area of environment, elements such as sound, light, temperature, and room design were all researched. Results found that although many children did not show marked preferences for some elements; for example, no sound versus sound in their learning environment, those who did show a preference were greatly influenced by whether or not their needs were met.

This research has led educators to examine at least twenty-one factors that could play a vital role in the development and learning of some children. Experiment after experiment revealed that when a child was having difficulty learning or adapting, if the teaching style was altered to closely match the child's preferences, the learning and behavior significantly improved.

One of the most influential factors in a child's learning is his or her *perceptual modality preference*. A perceptual modality is defined as the sense (hearing, sight, touch, experiential) through which a child learns most effectively.

Auditory children learn through hearing. They perceive their world through the sounds that come at them. These students listen attentively (unless they are familiar with the information, at which point they will most likely become bored). They rarely take notes or ask for a written copy, a map, or a pictorial presentation. The auditory teacher uses auditory language to communicate; for example, "Is everyone listening?"

Visual learners process information through sight. They "see" their world. They notice classroom decorations and are enthralled with videos, TV, books, pictures, and so on. They notice others' clothing as well as colors and designs. They watch what you do. The visual teacher uses visual language; for example, "I need everyone's eyes on me."

Tactual learners explore their world through touch. For them to grasp new and difficult information, they need to "get in touch" with the concept. For example, if you were trying to teach them the difference between "soft" and "rough," they would need to be presented with a piece of cotton and a piece of sandpaper. Feeling and comparing would bring about quick, effective learning. Tactual learners need to "feel good" about what they are learning. Whereas some children may not care if the information pertains to them, some tactual children find this an important aspect of the process. The tactual teacher will communicate tactually; for example, "Are you all grasping this information?"

Kinesthetic students prefer large body movement while learning. They prefer to actually experience the material. To grasp information they have to act it out; for example, using their bodies to become a "storm at sea." To experience learning, these children need to walk through a process to take in new and difficult information. For example, if they were making chocolate chip cookies, just hearing the instructions would not teach these children. Seeing the instructions would not make a lasting impression, just as touching a cookie would not help them learn. These children need to make cookies. The kinesthetic teacher communicates kinesthetically; for example, "Are you all getting into this?"

It is important to note that most of American education is geared to auditory/visual learners. We have very few apprentice or hands-on training programs at the early childhood and elementary levels.

Young children tend to favor a multimodal approach to learning. Indeed, all senses should be stimulated to encourage a full range of skills in the developing child. However, understanding the perceptual modality preference will help teachers understand the choices of some of their more difficult students.

How does this translate into the classroom? Consider Joshua, an *easy auditory* child. Teaching Joshua is a pleasant experience. He responds well to new situations and takes verbal instruction well. When the teacher says, "Joshua, it's story time. Come sit down," Joshua runs to take his seat, usually clapping enthusiastically.

On the other hand, Heather is a *challenging tactual* child. She throws a tantrum nearly every time she comes to class. She shouts "No!" when presented with toys that would help transition her into a new situation, and when she finally does settle in, she walks around touching, pulling, and knocking over everybody and everything in sight. This is the child who makes most teachers (and parents) understand why they need a good dose of patience and a healthy grasp of how to deal with the challenging tactual child. This brings us to step two in the easy-to-remember guidelines.

Develop a Flexible Plan to "Grow" a Healthy Child

A plan can be as simple or as complex as you have time to develop. The first step is to determine where the children who come into your class on a given day fall in terms of easy, slow-to-warm-up, challenging, or a mix.

After making that determination, assign students to staff based on the personalities of the staff. Teachers with easy children can handle a one-to-five or one-to-ten ratio with little difficulty. On the other hand, challenging children may require one-on-one attention. Matching children to staff is one of the most important responsibilities of the teacher or director.

The second step is to match the perceptual modality preference (PMP). PMPs are not as easy to match. To determine the PMP of your staff, monitor their conversations and interests. The table below will help you decide.

Perceptual Modality	Auditory	Visual
Perceptual Language (Phrase) Examples	• "I hear you." • "I'm listening." • "Everyone put on their listening ears."	• "I see." • "I see what you're saying." • "All eyes on me."
Tasks Enjoyed	• discussing • listening to students • debating • drama • listening to audio books • reading to students • listening to music	• seeing pictures • using facial expressions • looking at picture books • watching dramas • taking pictures of students • producing art • playing dress up • making models • coloring • illustrating • writing

Perceptual Modality	Tactual	Kinesthetic
Perceptual Language (Phrase) Examples	• "I'm connecting with you." • "You're touching on an interesting subject." • "I need to touch base with everyone."	• "I get what you're saying." • "I get it." • "Let's get onboard and pay attention."
Tasks Enjoyed	• acting in dramatic presentations • dressing up • touching objects • making models • making visuals • playing in sand or water tables • conducting a survey • playing charades • playing games • taking notes or coloring while you teach • working on computers	• moving while you teach • acting • exercising • playing games • moving in rocking chairs, on balance boards, or on stationary bikes while listening • working on computers • playing electronic games • taking field trips • participating in demonstrations

Once you have determined the staff's preferences (along with your own), encourage the staff to work with the students who seem to favor their kinds of perceptual modalities. Note: As adults, most of us have already learned to utilize all of the senses to learn. This makes for a capable staff. However, occasionally staffs are young and have not fully transitioned to making use of all their senses. When this is the case, intervene by matching each student's and staff member's perceptual modality. When the staff and students are in sync, move to guideline three.

Determine to Meet the Child's Needs by Understanding Your Own Strategies

Self-evaluation is always a valuable tool for the teacher. Research tells us that we tend to teach according to how we learn. For example, if you hear yourself demanding peace and quiet, your learning style probably includes low noise levels. At this point, it is valuable to read through an abbreviated list of elements that affect learning taken from Dunn and Dunn's model and decide what elements are important to you and which are not. Then look at your students and decide if your preferences are getting in the way of their learning. Below is a quick summary of the main elements. Also listed are resources in which to find research and work by specialists in these areas.

Regarding sound. Do you sing to yourself while you work or learn? Do you like music in the background? Do you read and watch TV at the same time? Are you able to concentrate while others talk? Do you prefer complete quiet while concentrating?

Regarding lighting. Do you need low lights or bright lights for learning? Do fluorescent lights give you a headache? Does the noise from fluorescent light irritate you? Do you prefer natural light?

Regarding room temperature. Do you need it to be cool or warm? Do you prefer a breeze or draft? Do you dress in layers? Are you constantly perspiring?

Regarding room design. Do you enjoy relaxing while you learn? Do you sit at a desk to do important work? Do you enjoy reading in a chair, on the floor, on a couch? Are you more comfortable in a formal or informal setting?

Regarding sociological needs. Do you enjoy learning alone or with others? Do you enjoy working in groups? Alone? With one or two friends? Do you like supervision when attempting a new project?

Regarding food and water. Do you tend to snack or eat when faced with new and difficult tasks? Are you constantly hungry? Do you look for opportunities to get something to drink? Do you have a favorite drink that you carry around constantly?

Regarding time. Are you at your best in the morning, afternoon, or evening? Do you tend to get up early without an alarm? Do you stay up late even when you got up early?

Regarding mobility. Do you like to pace when you're learning? Do you get up and do a chore when you're reading or working? Do you wiggle your feet while you're listening to a sermon? Do you change positions often? Do you get irritated with people who can't sit still?

Regarding perceptual modality. (See definitions above.) Since we tend to be most "comfortable" when others are like us, we may automatically respond to children most like us. When we begin to evaluate and understand our styles, we can develop strategies to deal with those who are different. After all is said and done, the teacher will still be responsible for meeting the child's needs by understanding his or her own strategies.

Demonstrate a Wide Range of Strategies to Meet the Child's Needs

It is important to keep two concepts in mind: (1) Let the children learn through their learning style preferences, and (2) expose them to other styles. Life is about transitions. Research shows us that children do not effectively transition from their style or preference until high school. That doesn't mean that they should be isolated from other styles. On the contrary, touch dominant children, for example, are going to have to operate in a primarily auditory/visual world. We would be doing them a disservice if we never exposed them or helped them transition to these major modalities.

Here are some ideas that may help your class:

Regarding sound and the learner. Divide the room into two groups—those who prefer quiet and those who like noise. Allow the "quiet needs" students to congregate in a corner of the room. Bring earmuffs, use partitions, or allow the students to bring their own earplugs. Allow instrumental music to play in the background for the group that prefers noise. Encourage the students to visit all areas.

Regarding lighting and the learner. This will depend on your classroom. Some room settings may allow the teacher to turn off the fluorescent lights and utilize natural lighting. Some rooms may need desk lamps, while others may need shades for the windows to cut down on light intensity. Students can have some control over their workstations by being allowed to wear hats to shield their eyes from annoying light. Generally, the younger the child, the less light intensity is necessary.

Regarding room temperature and the learner. Provide jackets, sweatshirts, or shawls—anything students can wrap up in. This also helps the touch dominant children with a tactual connection to their environment. For those students who are too warm, a fan may help. The outside edges of the classroom tend to be cooler than the middle of the room, but consideration of the heating and cooling vents is important.

Regarding room design and the learner. Move tables and chairs to one corner of the room and allow the students to lounge on the floor. Or if you are working in several rooms, use one as a "formal seat" work room and the other as a casual listening room, and rotate the students through the rooms.

Regarding sociological needs and the learner. This is a difficult need to meet in most church settings. Be careful to allow friends to stay and play together. Since young people tend to be peer-dependent, this is not the time to isolate them from companions so that you can have their undivided attention. You are apt to lose their attention and most likely their attendance as well.

Regarding food and water and the learner. Provide munchies and allow students to bring no-spill water bottles. Despite popular belief, sugar does not generally give students an adrenaline rush and predispose them to hyperactivity. Be aware of food allergies and special needs, but generally crackers, chips, and cookies are acceptable to serve.

Regarding time and the learner. Take advantage of the morning learners in your Sunday morning class. If the students appear to be getting drowsy, move to an action activity. Only about 25 percent of the population are naturally morning people. Children are no exception.

Regarding mobility and the learner. Balance boards, stationary bikes, running in place, moving around the classroom, slides, and large motor activity toys are all ways to help the kinesthetic learner. This child is required by our culture to transition into an acceptable style of classroom behavior, but you can help such students transition by being kind and giving them a variety of opportunities to learn.

Regarding perceptual modality and the learner. One of the most important things you'll ever do is learn about each student's perceptual modality. A child's modality will affect every aspect of his or her life. (See Perceptual Modality section.)

The learning style of a child is as individual as his or her fingerprint. I cannot say that each classroom will need to meet each student's needs. That would not be possible and would be unhealthy for the developing child who will have to learn to deal with incongruencies in life. What I can encourage is that as you deal with a difficult child or a child who does not "fit in," does not cope well, or is labeled as "difficult," you take into consideration the elements that you have some control over—specifically, the elements researched by Dunn and Dunn. Moreover, while you look at these elements, decide if there is anything you can do to help this child be a success.

Our role as Christian educators is to fulfill Christ's commands to make disciples. We can learn effective ways to do this.

Sources

Rita Dunn, Kenneth Dunn, and Janet Perrin, *Teaching Young Children through Their Learning Styles* (Boston: Allyn and Bacon), 1994.

Suzette Haden Elgen, *Try to Feel It My Way: New Help for Touch Dominant People and Those Who Care about Them,* (New York: John Wiley & Sons), 1996.

How Can I Make It Work?
Effective Lesson Planning

Now that you understand why curriculum is important, how it is developed, and what its elements are, you need to know how to make it work for you in the classroom. While the curriculum is designed to be teacher-friendly and provide all the content and creative activities you need to present a great lesson, the key to effective use is careful planning. There just isn't any way around it.

Whatever project you might tackle, from completing an artistic craft to building a home, the process begins with establishing a plan and following through with that plan. Essential to that process is gathering the necessary tools you will need to make it happen and then determining how those tools will be used to arrive at completion.

The overarching goal in Christian education is to help develop the spiritual lives of children, youth, and adults by teaching them God's Word and helping them apply it to everyday life. It is more than an instructional process; it is a transformational process that helps them to understand that Christianity is ultimate reality and to think and act in ways that are pleasing to God and exemplary to others around them.

Accomplishing any worthwhile goal requires careful planning. Part of that planning involves a thorough understanding and application of the tools that will help achieve the goal. Now that you have been given a thorough review of Radiant Life Resources, this chapter will help you put together what you have learned in the lesson planning process.

Advance Quarterly Planning—Getting the Big Picture

A major project, like building a home, requires taking a look at the big picture to see what the house will look like when it is finished. Attention isn't given to just the living room or the kitchen or the bathrooms. The whole floor plan is reviewed to give a complete overview of how the house will be laid out. Understanding the big picture is necessary to putting in place all the minute details of the project.

While beginning a new quarter of studies is not as major as building a home, it is an important part of building spiritual foundations in the lives of your students. So, once your Radiant Life resources are in hand, take time to review everything in your set of materials to get the big picture of what you want to accomplish during the quarter.

Here is a suggested procedure to follow as soon as you receive your materials for a new quarter:

1. Lay out all of the components—the teacher guide, student books, and resource packet items.

2. Scan through the contents of the entire teacher guide.

3. List the unit themes and weekly lesson topics on a sheet of paper to help lock them in your mind.

4. Read the Teacher Skill Builder article(s) that provide helpful in-service training.

5. Review the philosophy and goals information at the front of the quarterly, especially if you are using the curriculum for the first time.

6. Review the unit activities that are suggested. You will not be able to do all of them with your students. Consider one or two possibilities in this preplanning phase. List the activities and the supplies you will need to do them. This will help you avoid last-minute gathering of materials. Later it would be good to work through the activities before doing them in class. That will give you a feel for the amount of time needed and help you determine whether the activity will fit your students' interests and abilities.

7. Look over all the items in your resource packet. Instructions on the packet envelope or on information sheets inside the packet will provide an overview of the contents and how each item is to be used. Note the materials that will need to be duplicated. How many copies will you need? Some items may be used for student reports. Will visuals need to be punched out or assembled? Doing some of this ahead of time will help you avoid a last-minute rush.

8. Label a separate file folder for each lesson and place the resource items in the appropriate folders. Include visuals, work sheets, overhead masters, student book items, and other materials. This will give you ready access to the resources as you do your weekly lesson planning. As you prepare your weekly lesson plan, all you have to do is choose the corresponding folder and you're ready to go.

Although this planning will take a little extra time up front, it will save a lot of hurrying and scurrying on an already busy Sunday morning. Advance preparation can reduce the stress of teaching and give you a sense of confidence as you prepare the weekly lessons.

91

Spiritual Preparation

As you plan each week's lesson, take time to prepare spiritually. While that should go without saying, it's easy to slip into a routine of reading through the teacher guide, gathering all the materials, and going through the motions in class week after week. The difference between teaching Sunday School and teaching Sunday School effectively is spiritual preparation. Here are some pointers:

- Pray for each student in your class by name. Pray that God will give your students a desire to learn about Him and His Word. Pray that God will keep them in His care and protection.
- Pray that as you teach, the truths shared will penetrate their hearts and minds. As you get to know your students, focus your prayers on specific needs or circumstances. If physical, emotional, or spiritual problems become evident, pray that God will minister to them with His love and care.
- Pray that God will give you wisdom and patience as you deal with difficult students. Praying will help change them and your attitude toward them.
- Pray for the anointing of the Holy Spirit upon you as you teach. Teaching Sunday School is as vital a ministry as any other in the church; as such it requires an anointing to be effective. You are in a position of high responsibility as you declare biblical truths and principles, and the Spirit's anointing will enable you to fulfill your role with power, love, and authority.
- Spend time in God's Word devotionally and in study. Read your Bible daily. Pray for the Holy Spirit's guidance as you read. As you immerse yourself in the Word, it will become part of your spiritual fabric and your thought life, and it will help you in your spiritual growth and teaching ministry. You can rely on the Holy Spirit's faithfulness to bring to mind

passages that will help you deal with personal issues as well as answer questions with which others are wrestling.

• Incorporate lesson preparation as part of your devotional time each week. Focus on the Bible passages being dealt with in the lessons. Study and meditate on those verses and allow them to sink deep into your heart and mind. Be sure to review and learn the memory verse; if you expect your students to know it, you should be able to recite the verse as well.

Lesson Preparation

When should you begin your weekly lesson preparation? Unfortunately, for some teachers lesson preparation begins late Saturday evening or even on the way to church on Sunday morning. While our schedules are packed with myriad tasks throughout the week, a habit of last-minute planning usually results in frustration for the teacher and disinterest among the students. Avoid this at all costs. It is difficult to be adequately organized and confident when eleventh-hour planning is practiced. Spiritual preparation for the class session most certainly will be lacking under such circumstances.

Consider planning the next week's lesson on Sunday afternoon while that day's class session is still fresh in your memory. Take a few moments to reflect on what took place in class—the lesson presentation, student participation, use of curriculum resources, and so on. Sometimes it is helpful to audio or video record your class session for playback afterward. The important thing is to evaluate ways to make your teaching ministry as effective as possible. Be careful, however, not to expect more of yourself than is possible to achieve. Your best is all that God requires.

Focusing on the Lesson Elements

As you prepare your weekly lesson plans, give careful attention to the elements of the lesson as presented in the printed curriculum—the topic, objective, Scripture text, key verse, life application, checklist, lesson presentation, and evangelism. The topic, objective, Scripture text, and life application give background and purpose for what will be delivered in the classroom through the remaining elements.

Topic

The lesson topic or title identifies the subject matter to be presented. While that seems obvious, the topic closely defines, at a glance, the content to be shared. Just enough information is given to let you know what the lesson presentation is about.

At the beginning of a new unit of studies, review with the students all of the lesson topics within that unit. That will give them an overview of the unit and how the various topics tie into the overall theme. If an introduction to the unit is provided in the teacher guide, share that information with the students as well rather than jumping into the unit without presenting the big picture. Sharing background information and reviewing the lesson topics will provide context for the weekly studies.

If the lesson topic is printed on a poster, be sure the poster is displayed in the classroom. If not, write the topic on the board or present it through the electronic medium you are using. Doing so will help focus thoughts on the subject at hand as the students arrive.

Objective

Read the lesson objective and fix it in your mind. Think of it as your target. Everything done prior to, during, and after the lesson presentation should relate to the objective. You may find it helpful to write the objective on an index card or sticky note and place it where you will see it throughout your planning time. Refer to the objective regularly as you prepare.

As mentioned in an earlier chapter, you may find it helpful to adjust the objective to fit your particular situation. Your students' cultural or ethnic context or level of Bible knowledge may lead you to redirect the approach you will take. In most cases, however, the printed objective will be appropriate to a wide variety of contexts.

Scripture Text

Always remember that God's Word, not the printed curriculum, is your ultimate reference point and authority base for the study at hand. It is the textbook. Immerse yourself in the Bible background for each study. After you have the topic and objective in focus, read the Scripture text before reading through the rest of the printed lesson plan. Let it sink deeply into your heart and mind. As one writer put it, the Word must again become flesh in the life of the teacher. You have opportunity to make God's Word come alive as you present its truths to your students.

Consider referring to various translations of the Bible in your lesson preparation to gain additional light on the meaning of the passages with which you will be dealing. A study Bible also can help expand your understanding of key concepts and truths. Other resources such as commentaries, concordances, Bible dictionaries, and atlases will expand your understanding of the biblical passages involved and give you additional information to share with your students. Remember that teaching is as much a learning experience for you as it is a training experience for your students. Additional research and study will provide a wealth of helpful background for you to use throughout your teaching ministry.

Plan to involve your students in the Word as much as possible. Children, particularly in elementary through teen years, need to be encouraged to bring their Bibles to class. Even if incentives have to be used, such as points or prizes, it is worthwhile to develop a habit of carrying a Bible to church. Sadly, many children and youth (even some adults) struggle with finding their way around in the Bible. At the very least, have some extra Bibles in the classroom for students to use.

Reading passages aloud is one way to use the Bible in class. Be sensitive, however, to students who have difficulty reading to avoid embarrassing them. Encountering God's Word must not become a negative experience. Students also can be asked to scan a passage and answer questions based on what they have read. These activities often are suggested in the printed lesson plan and, if not, can be woven into almost any lesson presentation.

Key Verse

Memory verses or key verses are featured in all lesson plans. These serve a twofold purpose: to capture the essence or central truth of the study and to help build the students' store of Bible knowledge. Most lesson plans provide a variety of activities to help students learn the verses. Discussion of the verse also is included at some point in the lesson presentation.

Again, some incentives for learning the verses can be used at the children's levels. Learning the memory verses is an important way of instilling the major thrust of a lesson in the child's mind. It is important that you as a teacher learn the verses along with your students for the same reason.

Life Application

A vital aspect of Christian education is building moral, social, and spiritual character in the lives of students. As children, youth, and adults encounter God's Word and discuss issues that pertain to living the Christian life, character change often is at issue. That is why each printed lesson presents a life application. Keep that application in mind as you prepare and as you teach. It is particularly relevant to the life application segment of the lesson that calls for response to God's Word in everyday living.

Checklist

Each lesson presents a checklist of items that can be used for the lesson presentation. Obviously, you will not use everything recommended for every lesson. That is where individual planning comes in. However, note what is contained in the checklist and gather the items you want to use. As indicated earlier, separating student book and take-home items as well as preparing visual aids and posters and placing those items in folders or packets can save a lot of time in week-to-week planning.

Reviewing the checklists for all lessons at the beginning of a new quarter will give you an idea of the things you will need. Gathering some of the essentials well ahead of time also will help you avoid last-minute trips to the store or church resource center for supplies not provided with the curriculum.

Lesson Presentation

Upon reading the Scripture text and reviewing the objective and life application, carefully read through the body of the lesson presentation. Introductory information will provide background for the lesson. From that point, the lesson content is presented in an interactive, teacher-directed format that involves both commentary and a variety of activity options that engage the students in the learning process. While a lecture approach may be used, plan to use as many of the student involvement suggestions as possible. This will make learning come alive, improving interest and retention.

- Note the use of the resource items provided in the curriculum, including the student book materials. Based on the number of students you have, their learning styles, necessary cultural adaptations, and available class time, determine which resources and activities you can use and gather them.
- Work through hands-on activities beforehand, whether crafts or student book exercises. This will help you gauge how much time is needed for those activities and their levels of difficulty. Plan what you will do with students who finish their work more quickly than others. You might want them to move on to another activity in the student materials or work on a craft while the others finish.

- Focus on the life application and response segment of the lesson. Ask the Holy Spirit to help you relate that portion powerfully to your students. Special emphasis is given in most lessons to ways students can apply what they have learned in the coming week. Prayerfully consider where your students are in their spiritual growth and development, and plan to present the application/response emphasis accordingly. Responding to and acting upon what is learned is the chief aim of discipleship.

- Plan to teach from an open Bible as much as possible. If you need the teacher guide, place it close to your Bible for reference, but try to keep the Bible in hand or directly before you as you teach. This will reinforce to the students that what you are teaching is based on God's Word.

Evangelism

Oftentimes teachers assume that students in the Sunday School class already have received Christ as Savior. This is particularly thought to be the case with children and youth from church families. However, we must never make this assumption. There is no better context than the Sunday School classroom to present an appeal for students to receive Christ as Savior. As the Holy Spirit leads, give opportunity for this to take place. In an intimate, small group setting, students of all ages can experience the warmth of fellowship and the love of Christ. Pray that the Holy Spirit will reveal to you students who need to take this important step in their lives and that He will give opportunity for you to lead them to this life-changing experience.

Many lessons also lend themselves to encouraging students to evangelize outside the classroom. Keep that in focus as you prepare your lessons. Help students realize that the ultimate goal of Christianity is to bring others to Christ.

Evaluate! Evaluate! Evaluate!

Perhaps the most important part of lesson planning is taking time to reflect on what took place in the classroom after you have finished teaching. Did your students grasp the essential facts of the study and understand its principal truth? Did you give opportunity for the students to restate to you in some way what they learned? Have they been able to recite key points of information from one week to the next? Do you see any evidence of life change taking place?

Radiant Life curriculum intentionally focuses on evaluation at the end of each lesson. Give close attention to the questions raised in the evaluation segment and keep those in focus as you prepare and present your studies each week.

How Much Time?

Although you can invest as much time as you wish with lesson planning, it need not consume a lot of time during the week, especially if advance planning has been done as outlined earlier. You may want to give some time to lesson planning as part of your daily devotions. Or set aside time one day to zero in on that Sunday's lesson. Radiant Life curriculum provides an easy-to-follow lesson plan that clearly outlines the lesson segments and helps you know what the options are for the various activities.

Perhaps the following scenario will help you. Note that this is only one example and probably involves more time than you are able to give each week to lesson planning. Nevertheless, consider how you might approach lesson planning through the week rather than leaving it as a last-minute exercise. Ultimately, you need to determine what is best for you and your schedule.

Sample Scenario

Here is a day-by-day example of how one teacher of young adults approached a study titled "The Second Coming of Christ."

Sunday Afternoon

While skimming the lesson for next Sunday, I can't help but think about how interest in end-time events has grown among young adults in recent years. My students are no exception; they often can be heard discussing the latest books and movies dealing with this subject. I determine that this upcoming unit will spark much interest among them.

At the same time, I'm struck by the seriousness of the topic. It's so easy to give mental and verbal assent to the fact that Jesus is coming again yet lack the passionate conviction of what that means in our lives. I pause for a moment of prayer, asking God to use this lesson and this unit to motivate students toward a deeper walk with Him and a stronger commitment to share His Word.

Sunday Evening

Looking through the resource packet, I'm especially drawn to the case study "Home Alone." While it is an illustration that has been used many times, I believe it will work well in focusing our attention on issues of practical application. Following the directions in the teacher guide, I will use it at the beginning of the third main point. It will serve as a reminder of the serious issues Christ's imminent return causes us to face.

Monday

I've been thinking about a lesson objective: "To identify the two phases of the second coming of Christ and place our hope in His imminent return." I want to give special emphasis to helping my students develop a plan to respond in some way this week to the second coming of Christ (lifestyle change, witness to someone, etc.).

While I still want to touch on identifying and defining the two phases of Christ's second coming, the objective will help us focus on two important points I would like to cover: (1) All of us in the class need to live our lives with a clear sense that Jesus could come at any moment, and (2) we need a renewed commitment to help prepare those around us for Christ's return. The third main point will help us greatly in focusing on these points.

Tuesday

During the introductory portion of the study, I want to spend sufficient time analyzing how students respond to the news of Christ's coming. I think this is an important foundational discussion. Attitudes like fear and apathy must be dealt with in order for us to respond properly to the promise of Christ's return.

I like to spend time thinking about the life application portion of the lesson early in the week as well. I'm especially struck by a particular quote in the teacher guide. It reminds students that the events of Christ's second coming "should not evoke fear in the hearts of those who seek to live in obedience to Jesus." This serves as a good starting point to talk about how to properly respond to this promise—with obedience and renewed commitment. I will close the lesson by having students develop a specific plan for responding in the coming week to the imminent return of Christ. This might include making a lifestyle change or talking to a loved one about Christ.

It doesn't take long to fill out the lesson outline now that I have established the introduction and conclusion of the lesson. I am also able to identify quickly the particular points I will emphasize. Without realizing it, I have already done the bulk of the necessary preparation for next week's lesson.

Wednesday

I stop by the church office before Wednesday night Bible study to drop off the transparency "Time Line of End-Time Events," the information sheets "Views of the Resurrection" and "Views of the Rapture," and the case study "Home Alone" for duplication and preparation.

Thursday

I want to take another look at the third main point. This will receive the greatest percentage of class time. The case study leads well into the first question, which I have altered slightly to read: "How can a Christian be sure he or she is always ready for the Rapture?" How important it is that we regularly examine our lives to ensure that our commitment to Christ remains strong. I also appreciate the emphasis on accountability to one another. Many in our class live and work in environments that are hostile to spiritual values. We need each other's help and encouragement just as we need the hope found in looking forward to Christ's return.

Saturday

I have a few final preparations to make for tomorrow's lesson. I want to take another look at the information sheets. This is important explanatory information, yet I don't want to spend a lot of time on it. I do, however, want to be able to answer any questions clearly and concisely.

As I prepare to retire for the night, I'm excited about the lesson. I continue to pray that God will anoint me to teach in a way that will impact and challenge the students to look forward to Christ's soon return.

Lesson Planning 101

On an earlier end of the age-level spectrum, here is an overview for kindergarten teachers:

Get the Big Picture
- Scan the lesson title and the objective.
- Read through the memory verse and the Bible story as it is printed in the teacher guide.
- Read the Bible story and verse from your Bible.

Scan Your Activities
- Read through all the activities in a lesson. Note the ones that will work well with your class.

Pray About It
- Ask God to help you plan the lesson well.

- Ask God to help you present the lesson well.
- Ask God to use you to change lives.

Plan the Five Key Elements

1. *Bible story*. This is the center of each lesson. Choose how you will tell it. Will you use props? Actions? Role-play? Make learning about God's Word fun and memorable.
2. *Spiritual response*. How will you lead children in prayer and life application?
3. *Memory verse*. How will you help children learn the verse and apply it to life?
4. *Arrival time*. How will you get the class off to a good start? Simpler is better.
5. *Review activities*. How will you help children remember God's Word and apply it to their lives? See the activity rules that follow.

Know the Basic Activity Rules

1. *The Ten-Minute Rule*. Each activity will take about ten minutes. This estimate is based on one teacher and a class of ten students.
2. *The Spare Rule*. Always have a spare activity in mind. This takes care of activities that are shorter than expected. It also covers for activities that "bomb."
3. *The "First Things First" Rule*. If you really like an activity or think it is important, make it the first activity after the Bible story. That way you won't run out of time for it.
4. *The Variety Counts Rule*. Choose different types of activities. Try to include something for each child in your class, from the "sit-and-listen" child to the "wiggles-all-the-time" child to the "loves-to-talk" child.
5. *The Quick-Kid Rule*. Be prepared for the child who finishes first. Plan to let him or her start the next activity. Or plan a simple in-between activity such as drawing.

Pack It Up

- By Saturday night have all your materials ready and in the car or by the door.
- On Sunday get to church early so you are ready when students arrive.

While lesson planning need not be time consuming, intentional planning each week will make all the difference in your teaching ministry. It will give you a sense of satisfaction and confidence as you present each week's study. Your students will sense your preparedness as well and be more inclined to listen and interact. The effort you make toward effective lesson planning will be time well spent.

Why Is a Pentecostal Curriculum Important?
Presenting Our Doctrinal Distinctives

Today many of the tools we use—drills, screwdrivers, mixers, electric knives, and more—are cordless; they operate on batteries. They are convenient and versatile, not limited by a length of cord plugged into an outlet. Their effectiveness, of course, depends entirely on the strength of their batteries, their power source. A full charge is needed to operate at peak efficiency.

Throughout this book we have been examining curriculum resources as tools to be used in the ministry of teaching. Ultimately, however, our reason for using these tools is to help children, youth, and adults themselves to become tools—instruments in God's hand to do His will—to be witnesses, workers, and disciplers. No other purpose in life is higher. Their effectiveness in these responsibilities, however, depends on the level of spiritual power resident in their lives. Receiving that power is what Pentecost is all about.

Some have compared the difference the baptism in the Holy Spirit makes to batteries in a flashlight, but that analogy is not entirely accurate. A flashlight without batteries is completely useless. Many non-Pentecostal Christians in our world love the Lord deeply and are serving Him as effectively as they are able. They are not useless to Christ and His kingdom. However, they do not have the level of spiritual power Jesus intended for His followers to have. The baptism in the Holy Spirit provides power to witness and stand for Christ that is dynamic and unique. It is important to realize that Pentecost is not only a doctrine of the Church; it is a biblical reality. But the freshness and vitality of that truth eventually will be lost unless it is kept before our children, youth, and adults. The demise of Pentecost is always only one generation away.

That is why the Radiant Life curriculum scope and sequence weaves in studies at all levels that deal with the issues of the baptism in the Holy Spirit and Spirit-filled living. While this is not the only doctrine of significance, it is vital to the spiritual formation and strengthening of every believer.

Is using a Pentecostal curriculum really that essential? Isn't it possible to weave teachings on Pentecost into any Sunday School curriculum? Yes, it's possible but not easy; and unless intentional effort is made to do so, Pentecost is overlooked. It is a matter of deciding what we want. A familiar maxim states, "The proof of the process is the product." If we want a Pentecostal product (Spirit-filled believers), we must have a Pentecostal process that involves careful, systematic teaching about the baptism in the Holy Spirit and other Pentecostal doctrines.

Salvation is, of course, the most fundamental of all doctrines, and is required for one to receive the baptism in the Holy Spirit. The understanding and application of all other doctrinal and theological truths are dependent on having received Christ as Lord and Savior. Since the salvation experience can never be assumed of students, Radiant Life curriculum regularly encourages teachers and workers to present the plan of salvation to children, youth, and adults. The Sunday School classroom is a fertile environment for receiving Christ as Savior. In the smaller, more intimate setting of the classroom, students sometimes feel more comfortable opening their hearts and lives to Christ.

Once students have received salvation, it is important to encourage them to seek the baptism in the Holy Spirit. According to our statement of faith on the Baptism, we believe all Christians are entitled to, and should seek, the baptism in the Holy Spirit with the initial physical evidence of speaking with other tongues, according to Acts 2:4. This experience gives Christians power to witness by their lives and words. While the baptism in the Holy Spirit is by no means the only doctrine given importance, it is central to a believer's faith, worship, and spiritual growth. Through the empowering of the Holy Spirit, the Pentecostal church has grown, and continues to grow, exponentially around the world. The dynamic power to witness makes a powerful difference in a believer's service to God and His Church.

Teaching about Pentecost

The baptism in the Holy Spirit can be experienced at almost any age, from early childhood through senior adulthood. Children as young as age five have received the Baptism. Some adults have not received this blessing until late in life. Thus, it is imperative that even preschool children be introduced to this wonderful, life-changing experience. Here are some general guidelines on teaching about the Baptism.

Fulfillment of prophecy. Hundreds of years before the Day of Pentecost, God proclaimed through the prophet Joel, "I will pour out my Spirit on all people. Your sons and daughters will prophesy, your old men will dream dreams, your young men will see visions. Even on my servants, both men and women, I will pour out my Spirit in those days" (Joel 2:28,29). That prophecy was fulfilled by the events recorded in Acts 2.

107

The Holy Spirit is a person. He is not an "it." Sometimes children (and even adults) can be confused by different emphases on the *experience* of Pentecost and the person of Pentecost. While the Baptism is a spiritual experience, this blessing fills us with the presence of the Holy Spirit's person. Preschoolers and early elementary children can understand the distinction of the Holy Spirit as a person; upper elementary children can grasp the concept of the Trinity. They can understand that the Holy Spirit is equal to God the Father and God the Son.

No reason to fear. Knowing that the initial physical sign of the baptism in the Holy Spirit is speaking with other tongues, some children, and even youth or adults, will shrink back from seeking this experience. They fear losing control and doing something foolish. Speaking in a strange language is not something they are used to doing. God the Holy Spirit is gentle. Scripture pictures Him as a dove, the gentlest of birds. He does not come upon us in a manner that makes us do weird or strange things, and we do not disengage mentally and emotionally when we speak in tongues. The Holy Spirit knows us better than we know ourselves. He loves us and knows our personality and understands any fears we may have. He does not frighten or embarrass those who trust in Him.

The significance of tongues. Believers sometimes wonder why tongues is a necessary part of receiving the baptism in the Holy Spirit. Here are some insights that will help:

- *Speaking in tongues is repeated as a sign of the Baptism in Scripture.* On the Day of Pentecost (Acts 2), three signs accompanied the initial outpouring of the Holy Spirit—the sound of a rushing wind, fire, and speaking in tongues. However, after that time, the only sign of the Baptism that remained was speaking in tongues (see Acts 10:44–46; 19:4–6).

- *Speaking in tongues signifies complete control of the Holy Spirit.* James 3:3–12 describes the power of the human tongue. The tongue is our unruliest member, capable of terrible evil.

When a person receives the baptism in the Holy Spirit, his or her tongue is completely surrendered to the Spirit's power, signifying absolute submission to the work of the Holy Spirit.

- *Sincere desire.* In some cases young believers and older ones alike will seek the baptism to "belong," as if the Baptism were some requirement to be part of a club. Young believers also can be caught up in the emotion of the moment when God is moving in a service and mimic speaking in tongues in an effort to copy what others are doing. Unless this experience is sincerely desired for its purpose—to help them be strong witnesses and take a stand for Christ—seeking the Baptism will have no result. Children and teens need to know that the act of speaking in tongues is only a sign that they have been filled, not a spiritual gold medal or grand finale. Speaking in tongues must be conveyed only as the sign of the Baptism, not a signal that they have reached a spiritual pinnacle, nor that they are part of an elite group. Being baptized in the Holy Spirit is only the beginning of a wonderful spiritual journey.

- *Relevance.* Teens and adults particularly need to understand the importance of the Baptism to everyday Christian life. They need to know why a certain teaching is relevant to them before they will actively pursue applying it to their lives. Help them recognize that being Pentecostal is not a means of making them better than non-Pentecostals. Pentecostals don't have more of the Holy Spirit; the Holy Spirit has more of them. This increases the possibility of the Spirit communicating with them and helping them to fulfill God's will. Invite questions about the validity of Pentecost. Share your own story about your experience and how receiving the Holy Spirit has made a difference in your life.

- *No "formulas."* In some cases altar workers have attempted to help the process along by having seekers relax their tongues or say certain words or phrases over and over. There is nothing that can "make it happen" other than the sovereign move of the Holy Spirit.

- *Sufficient time.* Allow the person seeking to spend time in prayer offering praise and worship to God.
- *Not every experience is the same.* Some seekers may think they need to respond just like the person next to them. Though some people will be very emotional and demonstrative, others will be more quiet and passive. The Holy Spirit works with us individually.
- *Encouragement.* If a seeker does not receive the infilling during a season of prayer (and do not tell him or her otherwise if you are not certain), encourage that person not to give up, but to continue seeking the Baptism. Jesus will honor his or her sincerity. If the person clearly has received the Baptism, celebrate that moment with a special prayer of thanksgiving to the Lord. Let others know what has happened, and encourage the seeker to do the same.
- *Prayer language.* Help seekers understand that the Holy Spirit sometimes intercedes for others through us when we speak in tongues. Humanly, we may not know how to pray for another person or circumstance. In those instances the Spirit prays through us.
- *Continuation.* Encourage the believer who has been baptized to practice his or her new prayer language regularly, whether in church or during prayer times at home. We live in a world filled with evil influences. We need the power of the Holy Spirit to be fresh in our hearts and lives in order to live victoriously and have a righteous influence on others.

Modeling Pentecost

Children learn a lot through example. As someone once said, the Christian experience sometimes is better "caught than taught." Children pick up volumes of information and impressions when they listen to Mom and Dad pray at mealtimes or when they take time for prayer and Bible reading during devotions. At church they observe older children, teens, their Sunday School teachers, and other adults worship God in their own ways. Through hearing testimonies, children learn of the goodness of God and discover that He can be trusted.

They also learn a lot about Pentecost when they hear someone speak in other tongues, whether in worship or as an operation of the gift of tongues followed by interpretation. They come to see Pentecostal expression as a vital part of the worship experience and a way that God talks to His people. Children also learn that having the Holy Spirit in their lives can help them be better Christians and can empower them to tell others about Jesus.

As a Pentecostal teacher, model Pentecost in your own life. Children learn by example. Have your students ever observed you worshiping God in the Spirit in a church service? You can be sure they are watching. Help them see firsthand what Spirit-filled living is about. If you have not been baptized in the Holy Spirit, seek this tremendous gift as an example to your students and as an additional source of spiritual power.

Pentecost in Radiant Life Resources

Preschool

Formal training on Pentecostal themes begins in the Radiant Life's Preschool curriculum. One example is a lesson titled "God Helps Peter Preach." Children are introduced to the events of the Day of Pentecost by talking about how much fun birthday parties are when a lot of friends come over and there are fun things to do. On the Day of Pentecost, Jerusalem was filled with thousands of excited people who had come to celebrate God's love for them.

As the lesson unfolds, the teacher shares that Peter, who was sometimes scared, and his friends were praying in Jerusalem

111

when suddenly they heard a sound like wind blowing loudly. Then flames of fire appeared over the peoples' heads. After that, the people, including Peter, began to speak with new words. When that happened, suddenly Peter wasn't afraid anymore and was able to talk to the visitors who had gathered around to see what was happening.

This type of presentation allows preschool children to recognize that the Holy Spirit helped Peter not to be afraid. While they may not be ready to receive the Baptism themselves, they can be happy that God helped Peter preach the good news that Jesus loves all people. They can understand that the special events of the Day of Pentecost are why Peter could be bold.

By the time children reach kindergarten age (5 to 6 years), they are capable of receiving the baptism in the Holy Spirit. Though this may be more the exception than the rule, we should never assume a child is too young at this point to receive this experience. An approach that kindergartners can identify with is hearing how Jesus sent the Holy Spirit as a special helper. Before He returned to heaven, Jesus promised His followers that He would send His Spirit to be a helper for all believers. The Spirit would help them to tell others about Jesus and to live a life that pleases God. Kindergartners are able to grasp the concept of a helper, and they can understand God's people being given a new language when the Holy Spirit filled them with His power. However, most probably will not fully understand why they need to receive this experience for themselves. Nevertheless, it is important that they know the Holy Spirit's power is available to them too. Seeds of biblical truth planted early in life will one day bear rich fruit.

Early Elementary

As children enter their public school years as primaries (grades 1 and 2, ages 6 to 8), their ability to understand the person and work of the Holy Spirit is much greater. In a study titled "Fresh

Fire from Heaven," primaries learn that the baptism in the Holy Spirit is one of four key doctrines, the others being salvation, divine healing, and the second coming of Christ. Focus is on the Upper Room experience in Jerusalem. After teaching is given about the crowd hearing the disciples speak in various languages and Peter's newfound boldness to preach, primaries are told that this special gift of tongues is for them too. Peter declared, "The promise is for you and your children" (Acts 2:39). This experience is available to them for the same reason it was available for the early disciples—to give them power to tell others about Jesus. So primaries are personally invited to seek this wonderful infilling. The evidence of the infilling, they learn, is speaking in an unknown language as the Holy Spirit comes upon them.

Upper Elementary

Studies on the Holy Spirit at the Middler (grades 3 and 4, ages 9 and 10) and Preteen (grades 5 and 6, ages 11 and 12) levels focus on the promise of the Father and the Holy Spirit as our helper. The Holy Spirit resides within them helping them to witness and to take a bold stand for Christ. Both Middler and Preteen students are at a prime age to receive the Baptism. They are fully able to understand both the promise and person of the Holy Spirit and the importance of the Baptism.

By the time they reach fifth and sixth grades, children also can grasp a more in-depth historical significance of Pentecost summarized as follows:

> Just before the Day of Pentecost, many people had gathered in Jerusalem to celebrate the Passover, a time of commemorating Israel's release from Egyptian captivity. During that celebration, a first sheaf of wheat was presented from their fields as an offering to God. This signified the promise of a life-sustaining harvest of wheat that God provided for them in their homeland. After the Passover, the Jews returned to their fields to finish the wheat harvest. Fifty days later, when the harvest was complete, they celebrated again, this

113

time with fresh bread made from the harvested wheat. This celebration was the Feast of Pentecost. Pentecost literally means "fiftieth," indicating the number of days from the Passover to Pentecost.

After Jesus was crucified and resurrected from the dead, He remained on the earth with His disciples for forty days. Before He ascended back into heaven, He instructed His followers to wait in Jerusalem for the promise of the Father. On the tenth day, fifty days after Jesus had risen from the dead, the 120 disciples gathered in the Upper Room heard the sound of a rushing wind, saw tongues of fire rest above their heads, and began to speak in a new language. The promise had come.

God's Word describes Jesus as the "firstfruits," comparing Him to the sheaf of wheat that was offered to God immediately following the Passover feast. His death and resurrection signaled a promise yet to come. The Day of Pentecost was then the fulfillment of God's promise. And just as wheat is needed for daily bread to sustain us and help us grow physically, the presence of the Holy Spirit daily sustains us and helps us grow spiritually.

Upper elementary children can understand that the baptism in the Holy Spirit is important to their spiritual formation. By this time in their lives, many middlers and preteens will have witnessed teens and adults worshiping in the Spirit. If they are completely new to a Pentecostal church, they may only have heard about this experience but not witnessed it. In such cases it is important to go over the basic teachings very carefully to help clear up misunderstandings and misguided perceptions about Pentecostals and Pentecostal worship.

But can children actually experience the baptism in the Holy Spirit as a result of hearing lessons about it? Absolutely! A husband and wife teaching team at a church in Oakland, California, took their class on a Radiant Life adventure to explore the Holy Spirit. One week they opened the class with the question, "How many of you would like to be filled with the Holy Spirit?" One by one, some instantly and others more shyly, children raised their hands. Encouraged, the teachers began to explain more about the Holy Spirit and His special baptism. After the lesson, the teachers gathered around their students and prayed for the baptism in the Holy Spirit. Their answer came quickly. The wonder of God swept through the small room, and soon every child began to speak in a new heavenly language.

Did it make a difference? Indeed it did! One girl later testified, "I learned the Holy Spirit would give me power and strength and help with my problems. I know I can pray in tongues and have my prayers answered."

Another student exclaimed, "When things didn't go my way, I used to get angry. Not anymore."

These children understood that speaking in tongues is the initial physical sign of the Baptism according to Acts 2:4. They experienced that sign firsthand. They also realized that the Baptism made a difference in their lives, helping them pray more effectively and behave more appropriately.

Following the sixth-grade doctrine course *Foundations for Faith*, a church in Springfield, Missouri, conducts a special retreat for the children that emphasizes the baptism in the Holy Spirit. Over the years many children have received this wonderful gift during prayer time.

Youth

Teens have reached a point in life when they desperately need the power of the Holy Spirit operating in their lives. Increased independence and intense peer pressure can present formidable challenges to staying on course spiritually. The dynamic of the Holy Spirit is needed to help them be witnesses and to maintain a Christlike life.

One Radiant Life study for high school students titled "The Evidence of the Spirit," deals with the questions "What does it mean to be Pentecostal?" "How can I be baptized in the Holy

Spirit?" and "Do I have to speak in tongues to be baptized in the Holy Spirit?" Teens are helped to understand that the primary reason Jesus baptizes Christians in the Holy Spirit is to better equip them to fulfill the Great Commission. The need for salvation as a prerequisite to receiving the Baptism is emphasized. If they are saved, they need to know that the Pentecostal experience is for all believers and that all they need to do is ask Jesus for this wonderful promise. Teens also learn that they do not disengage mentally when they speak in tongues. Speaking in tongues is a sign repeated in Scripture as the evidence of the Baptism and also is evidence of the complete control of the Holy Spirit.

Adult

Even when believers move into their young adult and older adult years, there is a need to emphasize the baptism in the Holy Spirit. Some adults may attend a Pentecostal church for years before surrendering to the work of the Holy Spirit. They may have misplaced fears about the experience or a wrong understanding of what the Baptism is all about and why it is important. Those who already have been filled with the Spirit need to be encouraged to practice praying in the Spirit and to allow Him to intercede through them.

Adult studies on Pentecost in Radiant Life curriculum deal largely with historical and theological perspectives. For example, a study titled "The Day of Pentecost" explores the historic framework of the Feast of Passover and the Feast of Pentecost in Deuteronomy and the fulfillment of Joel's prophecy about the outpouring of the Holy Spirit. These provide a backdrop for studying the outpouring of the Holy Spirit on the Day of Pentecost recorded in Acts.

While many older adults already have received the baptism in the Holy Spirit, it cannot be assumed that all have done so. That would certainly be true of newcomers to the church, particularly recent converts. Also, those who have received the Pentecostal experience must be encouraged to continue to pray in the Spirit and allow Him to further develop them in their spiritual growth.

Power for Living

Emphasis must always be placed on the difference the presence and power of the Holy Spirit makes in our lives. Not only are we given greater boldness to witness, but also we are given strength to stand for Christ. The Holy Spirit gives us power to live a holy life. This is a crucial issue, especially for upper elementary and teen students who are moving into a period of life filled with temptations and distractions. Peer pressure will make taking a holiness stand a greater challenge than ever. They need the help of the Holy Spirit to face those challenges victoriously.

The Holy Spirit further enables all Christians to engage in spiritual warfare. As students move into the teen years and beyond, Radiant Life curriculum provides focused studies on this issue. Students are helped to realize that they must depend on the presence and power of the Holy Spirit to be victorious against Satan's attacks.

God the Holy Spirit also provides guidance as we trust in Him and study His Word. Jesus promised that His Spirit would help guide us into all truth (John 16:13). Believers of all ages need His help to fully understand and apply God's Word to life.

With the presence and power of the Holy Spirit dynamically present, believers should also begin to exhibit the fruit of the Spirit in their lives—love, joy, peace, patience, kindness, goodness, faithfulness, gentleness, and self-control (Galatians 5:22,23). While these are not contingent on the Baptism, experiencing Pentecost will energize believers as they develop spiritually.

A Powerful Prayer Language

A very important benefit of the Baptism is the special prayer language we receive. Often there are times when it is difficult to pray about some things because we simply do not know what to say or we feel completely inadequate to express the need. Sometimes when we kneel to pray, our minds are so cluttered by everyday life that our prayer is like a small trickle. But when we allow the Holy Spirit to pray through us, things are much different. He fully understands what we are going through or what someone we are praying for is experiencing. The Holy Spirit is able to bypass our own understanding and pray through us for those needs. Instead of a trickle, our prayer becomes a mighty river of praise to God and intercession on behalf of our need or someone else's. Many people testify of a refreshing and a sense of peace that follow praying in the Holy Spirit.

Children, youth, and adults should be encouraged to pray regularly in the Spirit. A one-time experience will not sustain their spiritual energy any more than eating a piece of bread once a week will keep them strong physically. Praying in the Spirit should be practiced often.

Gifts of the Spirit

Although receiving the baptism in the Holy Spirit is a vital spiritual experience, there is much more to living the Spirit-filled life. Both 1 Corinthians and Romans outline gifts of the Spirit available to believers. Beginning with the Preteen level, Radiant Life curriculum provides focused studies on those gifts to help students understand what they are and why they are important to the church.

One unit of study at the Preteen level on spiritual gifts provides individual studies on the baptism in the Holy Spirit, the knowing gifts (wisdom, knowledge, distinguishing of spirits), the speaking gifts (prophecy, tongues, interpretation of tongues), and the action gifts (faith, healing, miracles). While fifth- and sixth-graders may not be actively involved in the operation of these gifts (though it is possible), it is vital that they receive instruction regarding them. In many cases students at this age have witnessed the operation of the gifts in an adult worship service. Often they do not understand what is happening but recognize that such demonstrations are very meaningful to the congregation. Careful instruction at this point in life will help them avoid misconceptions and hopefully encourage them to actively seek the gifts of the Spirit in their own lives. They need to realize that the speaking gifts in particular are not emotional outbursts that originate with the person(s) speaking, but that those people are being moved upon by the Holy Spirit to convey a special message to the congregation.

As students move into their teen years, teachers sometimes find them skeptical, even cynical, about the operation of the gifts of the Spirit, particularly the speaking gifts. While misuse of the gifts sometimes occurs, teens need to realize their importance to the life and growth of the church individually and corporately. Teens are quite capable of being used in the gifts and should be encouraged to actively seek them.

Radiant Life teen and high school studies on the gifts help youth understand the gifts from a biblical perspective. They are helped to see that through all the gifts, God is able to speak and act in supernatural ways within His church. These studies give great relevance to the operation of the Holy Spirit in ways teens can appreciate.

While adults may be more advanced in their understanding of spiritual gifts, few may actually be practicing or actively pursuing them. At issue is a willingness to commit to the sovereign work of the Holy Spirit. In Radiant Life curriculum, adults, young and old, are encouraged to move beyond the experience of the baptism in the Holy Spirit and seek to be used in the gifts. This requires a full surrender on their part to the Spirit's work. Curricular materials are designed to highlight the value of the gifts and help Pentecostal adults recognize both their privilege and responsibility of being used by the Spirit to minister to God's people.

Perpetuating Pentecost

Perpetuating Pentecost must be an intentional process within the ministry of Christian education. Without ongoing emphasis on the baptism in the Holy Spirit and the operation of the gifts, there is great risk of losing sight of this distinctive altogether. Children, youth, and adults must be helped to recognize that the vitality of their church depends on the operation of the Holy Spirit, not just in the speaking gifts, but also in the areas of faith, knowledge, discernment, healing, and others. God has given those gifts to help strengthen the church through His super-natural intervention.

Of paramount importance in this effort is the use of a thoroughly Pentecostal Sunday School curriculum. While there are many choices of resources on the market, a non-Pentecostal curriculum simply will not convey or support issues related to Spirit-filled living. Though teachers may intend to insert such teaching at appropriate points, often it is difficult to judge when that should be done in a curriculum that does not support Pentecostal teachings. Radiant Life Resources endeavors to measure out Pentecostal emphases from early childhood through adulthood that will help children, youth, and adults mature in their understanding of Pentecostal distinctives and their relevance to everyday Christian life.

Radiant Life Q & A

8

Q: It seems like it takes a long time for suggested changes to appear in the curriculum. Why is that so?

A: Since our best curriculum consultants are those who use the materials week after week, every effort is made to respond as quickly as possible to suggestions from the field. Depending on their complexity, some changes can be made within quarters that are in various stages of the editorial and design processes; however, since curriculum is developed on a quarterly basis, it usually takes a full year for major changes to appear. Here's why: Once the outlines have been prepared, the editors assign writers to draft the content. Writers are given three months to complete their assignments. When the manuscripts are received, another three months are spent editing and designing the materials. Once the editorial team completes the electronic files, they are sent to the prepress area for preparation to print. To insure that churches have their curriculum in time, the resources need to be ready to order three months before the quarter begins. So, that completes a full year in preparing any given quarter. Major changes must be decided upon and implemented before assignments are made to writers.

Q: Who writes Radiant Life curriculum?

A: Assignments are made to Spirit-filled teachers, educators, pastors, and others who are experienced in working with the age level for whom they are writing. While the editorial staff does some writing, their task is primarily editing, which occasionally calls for restructuring.

Q: What if activities are too difficult or too easy for the children in my classroom?

A: Radiant Life curriculum is a tool. Select activities that fit the children in your classroom. If some seem difficult, help the children complete some of the steps. If your children are more developed, allow them to complete tasks you might normally have prepared in advance.

Q: Where can I find inexpensive equipment and supplies for my classroom?

A: Consider these options:
- Shop at garage sales for toys, dress-up clothes, art supplies, and other equipment.
- Bring materials from home.
- Check with church leadership about having a church shower to supply the room.
- Post a list of needed items and encourage parents and church members to donate them.
- Check with public school teachers in your church to see if there is a resource supply center in your area where inexpensive materials may be obtained.

Q: Why should I buy student resources? Sometimes there isn't enough time in class to use them.

A: Planning ahead is always the key. As you are working through your lesson plan each week, take a close look at the student book items and see how they will best fit into your lesson presentation and schedule. Don't feel like you have to do everything. Certain activities will take more time than others, especially if you have some students who are very meticulous in their work. Let students work together on activities in the student materials, especially on exercises that involve code-breaking or unscrambling words and sentences. Working together helps build relationships and moves things along more quickly in class. You may also have students work on different activities rather than having everyone do them all. Also consider asking students to work on the activities in the student materials a week ahead of time and bring their answers back to class. Offering incentives such as points or a prize can help them remember to complete the activities.

Q: Why are the Sunday School lesson themes repeated in the preschool children's church materials?

A: Young children focus best on one idea at a time. Radiant Life keeps this childhood trait in mind by continuing one theme throughout a morning's sessions. Children's church is a time of reinforcing truths learned in Sunday School and an opportunity to practice biblical principles through active learning.

Q: How can I make repetition of Bible themes exciting in children's church?

A: Children's church is an opportunity to teach the way a child learns best—through active learning. Vary the schedule. Consider opening with learning centers. Use a variety of short activities to reinforce the Bible theme. Use the Sycamore Sam character. Children enjoy helping Sam retell the story, holding props for him, and reminding him of what happens next in a story.

Q: Why are Bible visuals for Sunday School and children's church the same?

A: Because Bible stories use the same Bible text, characters are the same in the stories at both levels. Using the same visuals enhances retention and allows children to participate in telling the story and placing the visuals.

Q: For what ages of children is the Kindergarten curriculum designed?

A: Children ages 5 and 6 who are not yet in first grade.

Q: For what ages of children is the Primary curriculum designed?

A: Primaries are children in first and second grades. The curriculum may also be adapted for use with children in third grade. However, Middler curriculum is specifically targeted for children in third and fourth grades.

Q: What if I have a small class of children from ages 5 through 7? Which curriculum should I use?

A: Try using the Kindergarten curriculum, which is designed to teach prereading skills. Or use the Primary curriculum with Primary One student guides. Either option can work if a teacher provides activities for the varying skill levels. Letting the older children be helpers for the younger children increases the chances of classroom harmony in this situation.

Q: How do I order supplies for a class that has twelve Primary children on the roll but a weekly attendance of only seven or eight? Do I order twelve of each of the student publications? Or can I order eight or nine instead?

A: Our student items are designed for weekly use, so you can order eight or nine copies. Pages in student books and the handwork packet are perforated for easy removal. The take-home story paper is printed in four-page weekly parts that pull apart.

Q: For what ages of children is the Middler curriculum designed?

A: Children in grades 3 and 4.

Q: Is Radiant Life Youth curriculum recycled in the same way as children's curriculum?

A: Not entirely. Although the Youth curriculum is built on a four-year cycle, current themes and issues that youth face are evaluated as each cycle reaches completion. Some themes naturally warrant repeating; however, certain contemporary issues need to be addressed in our constantly changing culture. Since Scripture is relevant to any time and circumstance, God's Word can be used to address concerns and interests that arise.

Q: Why don't the titles in the *High School Spirit* and *Young Teen Study Guides* match the titles in the teacher guides?

A: The study guides are intended to inspire, intrigue, and capture the attention of teens, not just be a rehash of the lesson. We want the study guide story to serve more as a sermon illustration or anecdote. These stories are often more memorable than the exposition, and students will read them instead of tossing them carelessly aside.

Q: Why are the *High School Spirit* and *Young Teen Study Guides* not stapled?

A: The study guides are not bound because they are not actually books to be handed out to and kept by the students. Although they are bundled together, they are individual sheets to be handed out each week, making them more convenient, cost-effective, and useful discipleship tools. The loose-page format eliminates the need to buy extra copies for students who lose their student books at home. You may want to have a few extra copies on hand to give to visitors or irregular attendees when they come or to mail to absentees. The ultimate goal is a cost-effective way to ensure that every student has a study guide each week that reinforces lesson truths and encourages them to apply what they have learned to their everyday lives.

Q: What do I do if I don't think a certain lesson or unit of study applies to my Youth class?

A: Consider using *Hot Traxx* from the High School or Young Teen resource packet as a lesson alternative (complete with activities and work sheet) for those times when a certain lesson just doesn't seem appropriate. The topics covered are meant to be timely and relevant. If you don't use them, be sure to save them for use at a future time. If you're looking for an entire unit on a specific subject and can't wait for it to appear in the dated curriculum, consider using one of the Real Life Youth elective series. These include titles on doctrine and foundational truths such as the Holy Spirit and the end times, as well as relevant topics that matter to teens.

Q: What is the difference between the *Connections* Adult curriculum and the Adult Teacher series?

A: *Connections* is an alternate Adult curriculum that can be used with any adult class; however, it is probably most compatible with young adults. Patterned after the adult Bible fellowship model, *Connections* provides an interactive discussion format in which the teacher serves more as a facilitator than lecturer (although a lecture format may be used). *Connections* explores a variety of contemporary topics and themes along with a balance of Bible book studies and doctrinal emphases.

The Adult Teacher series is based on a seven-year cycle that takes students through a complete overview of the Bible from Genesis to Revelation. This curriculum is largely expositional in content and accommodates more of a lecture format; however, a number of discussion questions and illustrations are incorporated to encourage student interaction.

Q: Some curricula have students at all age levels studying the same topics. Why doesn't Radiant Life follow that approach?

A: Unified lesson themes have been popular in some circles, and the concept of having everyone on the same topic sounds logical. The greatest shortfall in this approach is the limitation it places on the scope and sequence of themes and topics. Many themes that are relevant to teens and adults (for example, doctrinal studies, prophecy, spiritual warfare, human sexuality, end-time events, etc.) would not relate well to preschoolers or even to early elementary children.

Radiant Life does provide a unified focus on Pentecost Sunday. Each year studies on the theme of Pentecost are included from preschool through adult. Also, seasonal studies such as Easter and Christmas are carried across the age-level spectrum.

Q: How can I involve adult students more effectively when teaching the lesson?

A: One reason some adults don't become involved is that they feel the teacher is the source of information. Making assignments for students to do ahead of time outside of class is one way to overcome this. This might be as simple as having them present a reading on a certain topic or theme. Also, pose nonthreatening, easy questions to students from time to time in class. Once your students become more comfortable with speaking in class, it will be easier to engage in discussion in the future.

Q: Most students in my adult class have been Christians for years. How do I make lessons that cover basic Bible knowledge interesting and applicable to them?

A: First, get the students involved in the lesson. Teaching tips and resource packet items are a good way to start this process. Also draw on the life experiences of the students, allowing their input to help you tailor the lessons to their needs. If they want to dig deeper into the Scriptures, you might want to try the Spiritual Discovery series elective studies. These are designed for students who want to discover for themselves what the Bible says. It involves outside preparation by the students, but if they are mature, Bible-studying believers, they will welcome the opportunity to study God's Word in a systematic way.

Q: What about electives? When should I use them?

A: Radiant Life Resources provides a number of elective studies for youth (Real Life electives) and adults (Spiritual Discovery series and Biblical Living series). Hundreds more are available on the general market. Whenever considering electives, the important issue is balance. With so many possibilities in terms of topics and themes, there is a tendency to fall into a "flavor of the month" pattern where topics are chosen simply because they sound interesting or are best-sellers. While many helpful and engaging topics are provided, electives should not be substituted entirely for the intentional, systematic study of God's Word that a dated curriculum provides.

When electives are used, give careful consideration to the learning and spiritual needs of the students. Will departing from the scope and sequence of the dated materials help them in their spiritual development? If so, consider how a list of elective topics might fit into a scope and sequence. In such a case, insert the elective into the instructional plan and then return to the dated sequence afterward. Note that electives often vary in length. Some will cover a typical thirteen-week quarterly period; others may have only eight or ten chapters. In those cases, you may need to spend more time on some studies if you want to stay on a quarter system.

Q: Are there any elective studies for children?

A: Yes. *Foundations for Faith* is a doctrine course especially designed for upper elementary children. During this fifteen-study course, students learn the fundamental beliefs of the church and the accompanying Bible verses. The course includes a leader guide with detailed information on the various doctrines; a student guide with both homework and class work sheets; and a resource packet with posters, work sheets, information sheets, and a cassette with songs and dramatizations. *Foundations for Faith* provides an ideal opportunity to help preteen students understand what they believe and why they believe it.

Q: What electives are available to youth through Radiant Life?

A: Four dynamic elective studies in the Real Life Youth elective series are provided for teens that help strengthen their relationship with God and apply biblical standards to real-life situations. Each study contains five or more studies for leaders and reproducible materials for teens: *The Holy Spirit: Power Source; To Infinity and*

129

Beyond: The End Times; *Facing My World* (covers issues of family and school violence, legislating morality, and international war); and *Different, but Alike* (examines prejudice and provides a scriptural response to racial, physical, sexual, and economic differences).

Since these electives contain only a few studies, they can easily be inserted as a unit of study, if desired, within a particular quarter.

Q: What elective studies are available for adults?

A: The Spiritual Discovery series provides thirty-one titles grouped into four major categories: Foundations (essentials for Pentecostal growth), Book Studies (to sharpen scriptural knowledge and study skills), Life Issues (relationships in the family and the church), and Critical Concerns (hard-hitting looks at today's issues).

Designed for interactive study, these electives give students the opportunity to engage biblical truth and its relation to their lives. Study guides are designed as workbooks, providing discussion topics followed by thought-provoking questions with exercises to reinforce the theme. The leader guide provides work sheets, overhead transparency masters, information sheets, and case studies.

The *Truths for Life* doctrine and discipleship study is a video-enhanced doctrine course that transmits core Pentecostal truths through thirteen short dramas and teaching segments that explain the foundations and essence of Pentecostal belief. The student guide features video review questions, life application activities, and in-depth Bible passages. The leader guide provides suggested answers for every student guide question; mini-lectures with supplemental information; suggested seminar formats, complete with detailed schedules; and a reproducible completion certificate.

The Biblical Living series includes four courses that touch on discipleship and mentoring:

- *You and Your Priorities* teaches how to prioritize life—including career, finances, time management, involvement in ministry, and leadership responsibilities.
- *You and Your Family* examines principles that will help strengthen and deepen relationships with parents, siblings, spouse, and children.
- *You and God* explores what the Bible has to say about our relationship with the Lord. Emphasis is given to getting the most out of personal devotions, how to be led by the Holy Spirit, and how to live in God's will.
- *You and Others* teaches how to develop healthy relationships, strengthen those relationships with godly and beneficial communication, gain a heart to serve others, and win others to Christ.

Q: Is team teaching a good option?

A: Yes. Having a partner in class, whether your spouse or a friend, can be very helpful. Responsibilities can be divided and/or rotated among teaching, record keeping, discipline, and activities. Also, if one teacher has to be absent, the other can cover the class without having to arrange for a substitute.

Team teaching also capitalizes on individual strengths and involves more people in the Sunday School ministry. Some church members would never consider teaching a lesson but are very creative with activities and vice versa. They are glad to help in Sunday School if they can work in their area of strength.

Q: In addition to the curriculum, what kinds of resources will assist me in lesson preparation?

A: A number of helpful resources should be considered for every teacher's library. Here are some suggestions:
- **Bible versions:** Comparing various Bible translations and

131

paraphrases can help shed light on the meaning and application of Scripture passages. Mainstays include the King James Version, New International Version, *New American Standard Bible*, and *The Living Bible* paraphrase. The Contemporary English Version is often used in children's curriculum.

- **Concordance:** If you are tracing a particular theme in Scripture or if you can remember only a key word or phrase in a verse but cannot recall where it is found, a concordance is very helpful. *The NIV Complete Concordance, Cruden's Concordance* and *Strong's Exhaustive Concordance* are three well-known resources. Most Bibles have a brief concordance in the back.

- **Bible dictionary:** A Bible dictionary will provide definitions of names and terms used throughout Scripture. *Unger's Bible Dictionary* is one of the most commonly used texts.

- **Bible encyclopedia:** A wealth of in-depth information about Bible characters, locations, topics, and themes can be obtained through a Bible encyclopedia. *The Zondervan Pictorial Encyclopedia of the Bible* and the *International Bible Encyclopedia* provide extensive information.

- **Bible atlas:** Understanding both the geography and culture of Bible lands is important to both teaching and learning. An atlas will provide maps from various periods of Bible history as well as information about the geography and culture during those times. The *Westminster Atlas of the Bible* is a helpful resource.

- **Computer software/Internet:** All of the above tools are included on various computer software packages, making research and lesson preparation much easier than combing through a number of texts. Information about both printed resources and software offerings can be obtained by checking the Gospel Publishing House website <www.gph.org> or by calling the toll-free line (1-800-641-4310). Various Internet sites such as <www.ag.org> and <www.radiantlife.org> can be used for research as well.

Q: What kinds of teacher training helps are available to me?

A: The Teacher Skill Builder articles included in each quarter's teacher guide are an ongoing resource for the Sunday School teacher. These deal with a variety of themes from lesson planning to classroom discipline to age-level characteristics and more. Additionally, numerous training resources, such as the one you are reading, are available through the national Sunday School Department, including publications and videos that focus on a wide range of topics. Information on those resources can be obtained by contacting the national Sunday School Department website <www.sundayschool.ag.org> or through the Gospel Publishing House website <www.gph.org>.

Q: What does Radiant Life provide for children's church?

A: Radiant Life provides two children's church programs—*Beginning Explorers*, for preschool children ages 3 to 6 (not in first grade), and *Young Explorers*, for elementary grades (ages 6 to 12).

Beginning Explorers is a dated children's church curriculum that correlates closely with the Preschool Sunday School lessons. Since young children learn best by focusing on one idea at a time, the same Bible text and theme are carried from Sunday School through children's church. Children's church for preschoolers is a time of reinforcing truths learned in Sunday School. Also the children are given opportunity to practice biblical principles through active learning.

The *Beginning Explorers* curriculum includes a leader guide, visuals, a kit with posters, pictures, stickers, flash cards, music CDs, etc. Additionally, Rusty and Raspberry and Sycamore Sam puppets can be used with various stories.

Young Explorers is an undated children's church curriculum that is presented in a thirteen-lesson format for use on a quarterly basis. Seventeen themes are available that deal with a wide variety of Bible topics and issues, including New Frontiers: Lessons from Joseph and Moses; Castles and Kings: Lessons from Old Testament Kings; Olympic Training: Lessons in Christian Living; Gladiator: Lessons about God's Armor; Super Sleuth: Lessons on the Holy Spirit; and more. The curriculum package includes a leader guide, resource pages, posters, a music cassette, music transparency masters, reproducible activity sheets, and a full-color theme backdrop transparency. Music CDs are also available.

Young Explorers is a flexible curriculum that can be adapted to accommodate a large or small children's church, with children from kindergarten through sixth grade. It can be used on Sunday morning or evening or on Wednesday evening, whenever a program is needed that is suitable for a large or small group of boys and girls of varying ages.

Q: Sometimes my students seem completely disinterested in the lesson. How can I help increase their interest and participation?

A: First of all, think about your lesson preparation. Do you develop a lesson plan each week and follow it? Last-minute or haphazard planning is generally quite evident to both you and your students. In your planning, consider how you will engage the students. What questions might you ask, or what activities could the children do to reinforce the content? The teacher guide provides a number of helps and options for you to consider.

Vary the way you present the lesson content, whether or not options are suggested in the teacher guide. For example, many lessons lend themselves to role-play scenarios. Children and youth enjoy this form of lesson presentation. Not only does it actively involve them, but also it helps reinforce both the facts and application of the study.

Have students look up key Bible verses in sword drill fashion. This is a good exercise in finding their way around the Bible.

Invite a guest speaker on occasion. This is especially effective with studies dealing with divine healing, salvation, the baptism in the Holy Spirit, and witnessing. Real-life testimonies or personal experiences can add a powerful perspective.

Avoid teaching directly from the teacher guide if possible. Hold the Bible as you teach. This will help your students recognize that God's Word is the base from which the lesson is drawn. If you need notes, insert them in the pages of your Bible.

Continually evaluate your teaching approach. Note the evaluative questions and statements at the end of each study.

Develop good relationships with your students. This requires contact beyond the Sunday School session. Getting together with your class socially for parties or outings will help you build important bridges to your students. You will gain perspectives on their lives and they on yours, which is difficult to accomplish during the relatively brief Sunday School class time. When your students know you care about them and take a personal interest in their welfare, their respect for you as a person and as a teacher will grow.

Q: How can I help my students apply to daily living what they are learning in Sunday School? How can I know life application is happening?

A: Discipleship, or living out what the Bible teaches, is a vital component of Christian education. Learning is only half the process; applying is the other half. Though learning is easier to measure and evaluate than discipleship, Radiant Life curriculum includes both a Life Application and a Taking It With Me emphasis in each lesson to help you know that life change is taking place. The Life

Application emphasis focuses on issues of character or moral development in relation to the lesson. Taking It With Me gives suggestions for ways the students can do something—in some cases even that week—to put the lesson into practice. Teachers also are encouraged to follow up the next Sunday to see if students have applied the prior week's lesson in some way.

Suggested Bible Verses for Memorization

Foundational Verses

About God
Genesis 1:1; Genesis 1:27;
Psalm 46:1; John 1:1; James 1:17

About Jesus
Luke 19:10; Philippians 2:9–11;
Hebrews 13:8; John 15:5

About the Holy Spirit
Acts 1:8; Romans 8:26; John 14:26;
John 16:13

The Trinity
Luke 3:22

What God Reaches Out to Give

Salvation: Jesus
John 3:16,17; 14:6; Luke 19:10;
Acts 4:12; Romans 6:23; Ephesians 2:8

Holy Spirit
Acts 1:8; 2:38

The Word
John 1:1; Hebrews 4:12;
2 Timothy 3:16; Psalm 119:105

Blessings
Philippians 4:19

Comfort
Psalm 23:1-4; 34:17,18; 55:22

Hope
Jeremiah 29:11

God's Love
John 3:16; 1 John 4:9

Peace
John 14:26,27; Philippians 4:6,7

Protection
Joshua 1:9; Psalm 121:2

Strength
Psalm 46:1; 1 Corinthians 10:13;
Philippians 4:13

Forgiveness
1 John 1:9

End Times

Eternal Life
John 11:25; 14:2,3;
1 Thessalonians 4:16

Rapture
1 Corinthians 15:52

Second Coming
Revelation 22:12

Judgment
Matthew 25:45,46;
2 Corinthians 5:10

New Heaven/Earth
2 Peter 3:13

Why We Need Salvation

Sin
Romans 3:23; 6:23

Receiving the Gift of God

Salvation
Romans 1:16; 10:9; 2 Corinthians 5:17;
Galatians 2:20

Developing a Relationship With God

Devotion to the Word Psalm 119:11; James 1:22; 2 Timothy 3:16	**Worship** Psalm 19:14; John 4:24; Romans 12:1,2
Praise Psalm 48:1; 139:14	**Commitment** Jeremiah 29:13; Galatians 6:9
Prayer Matthew 7:7,8; Ephesians 6:18; Philippians 4:6; 1 Thessalonians 5:17; James 5:15	**Love God** Luke 10:27; Romans 8:28
	Church Psalm 122:1

Follow-up to Salvation

Communion 1 Corinthians 11:26	**What to Think About** Romans 12:1,3; Philippians 4:8
Water Baptism Romans 6:4	**Wisdom** James 1:5
Holy Spirit Acts 2:4; 2:38	

Living in the World

Adversity Psalm 46:1; James 1:2,12	**Fear** Joshua 1:9; Psalm 34:4; 46:1; Isaiah 41:10; Hebrews 13:6; 2 Timothy 1:7
Anger Proverbs 15:1; Ephesians 4:26; James 1:19,20	**Temptation** 1 Corinthians 10:13
Anxiety Isaiah 41:10; Philippians 4:6,7; Hebrews 13:6; 1 Peter 5:7	**Pride** Proverbs 16:18
Depression Psalm 34:17,18	**Tongue** Ephesians 4:29; James 3:9,10
	Revenge Romans 12:19

Characteristics of a Life in Christ (Sanctification)

Faith Ephesians 2:8; Hebrews 11:1,6; James 2:17	**Obedience** John 14:15; Ephesians 6:1
Fruit of the Spirit: Galatians 5:22,23	**Ten Commandments** Exodus 20:3-17
Caring for Self 1 Corinthians 6:19	**Thankfulness** Psalm 136:1
Character 1 Samuel 16:7	**Trust** Proverbs 3:5,6
Guidance Psalm 37:4; Proverbs 3:5,6; Matthew 6:33	**Commitment** Philippians 3:14
Humility Philippians 2:3,14	**Will of God** 1 John 2:17
Holiness Hebrews 12:14	**Contentment** Philippians 4:11; Hebrews 13:5
Giving Malachi 3:10; Luke 6:38; 2 Corinthians 9:7	**Victory** Romans 8:37
Peace Romans 5:1; Philippians 4:7	**Attitude** Philippians 2:5

Witnessing / Evangelism / Lifestyle

Testimony 1 Peter 3:15	**Love of Others** Matthew 7:12; John 13:34,35; - Ephesians 4:32; 1 Corinthians 13:13; 1 John 4:8
Ministry and Missions Matthew 28:19; Mark 16:15; 1 Peter 4:10	
## Signs and Wonders	
Healing Isaiah 53:5; Matthew 19:26; James 5:13–16	**Forgiveness** Matthew 6:14; Ephesians: 4:32

Suggested Passages

The Lord's Prayer Matthew 6:9–13	**The Days of Creation** Genesis 1
The Lord Is My Shepherd Psalm 23	**The Books of the Bible**
The Love Chapter 1 Corinthians 13	**A Psalm of Gladness** Psalm 100
The Ten Commandments Exodus 20:3-17	**The Lord Hates These Things** Proverbs 6:16–19
The Romans Road of Salvation Romans 3:10,23; 5:12; 5:8; 6:23; 10:17; 10:9,10,13	**Salt and Light** Matthew 5:13–16
The ABCs of Salvation Romans 3:23; John 3:16; 1 John 1:9	**The Birth of Jesus** Luke 2:4–7,11–18
Jesus' Disciples Matthew 10:2–4; Mark 3:16–19; Luke 6:12–16	**A Time for Everything** Ecclesiastes 3:1–8